Expressing th[e]
and Unrepea[table]

THEOLOGY
OF STYLE

LILLIAN
FALLON

ASCENSION
West Chester, PA

Nihil obstat: Deacon Christopher May
           Censor librorum

Imprimatur: +Most Reverend Alfred Schlert
           Bishop of Allentown
           May 8, 2023

Ascension
PO Box 1990
West Chester, PA 19380
1-800-376-0520
ascensionpress.com

Cover design: Faceout Studio

Printed in the United States of America
23 24 25 26 27 5 4 3 2 1

ISBN 978-1-954882-13-3 (paperback)
ISBN 978-1-954882-14-0 (e-book)

Contents

Introduction

DOES WHAT WE WEAR ACTUALLY MATTER?

Should Catholics care about what they wear?

The obvious answer is "yes." The clothing we wear is undoubtedly important. We wouldn't wear sweatpants to meet the pope, for example, which means clothing ourselves requires an understanding of appropriateness for our environment. In fact, the way we dress is another way we reveal our perennial call to self-gift.

But what about "style"? What do you think of when you see or hear this word? What images does it conjure up? What is a "stylish" person to you? Perhaps the pages of certain fashion magazines are going through your mind, or maybe television shows of dressing room montage scenes are flashing before your eyes. "Style" is more than just throwing on appropriate clothing for a particular occasion. Style is methodical, artful, expressive, and intentional.

For many, however, style is the superfluous cousin of practical dressing. It is not really necessary, but it *is* nice—right? Who doesn't love "oohing" and "ahhing" over a cute outfit? Some of us might even feel a pang of guilt after splurging on a particularly lovely dress, wondering how an inanimate object could capture our fancy with such force. We scold ourselves saying, "I should have bought something more practical! I care too much about how I look!"

It is easy to appreciate what is stylish, but it can be hard to justify its importance—especially when we are rightfully encouraged by the New Testament to not place too much value in material things.

But what if I told you that this innate pull toward certain items of clothing is actually a sign of being made in the image and likeness of God? I know, this sounds like a bit of a leap, but trust me, it checks out. Before you spend your life savings at the mall, this is not an excuse to become a shopaholic!

It is natural for humans to gravitate toward beauty. We see this in our attraction to great works of art and music, as well as our appreciation for God's vast creation. But what makes style unique is that it combines the beauty of a material item with the beauty of the human person. In this creative act, the beauty of a garment unites with the beauty of a person's identity and emphasizes her unique personhood.

Personal style is not commonly associated with growing in faith. Seen through a theological lens, however, it can be a tool for building our relationship with God. In his Theology of the Body, St. John Paul II masterfully provides an explanation for how man is made in the image of God. A "theology of style" shows how we live out being made in the Image every day—even in simple things, such as how we dress. An awareness of this truth allows us to have a greater understanding of our human anthropology, transforming how we see ourselves and our Creator.

You are probably thinking, "So, I can arrive at this life-changing knowledge through something as simple as personal style?"

I know this sounds simplistic and maybe even strange, but making big personal changes often begins with small, daily choices. Of course, radical self-discovery must be fueled by the desire to know who God is.

As Catholics, we are familiar with the power of someone's testimony. I have always found that the most impactful messages come from personal stories, so I will begin by illustrating my own journey from fashion-obsessed teen to theology-conscious adult.

Part 1

FASHION GIRL IN A CATHOLIC WORLD

*C*lothes and fashion are materialistic, I thought, as I switched between website tabs for the Fashion Institute of Technology (FIT) in New York and Ave Maria University. Absentmindedly tapping the keyboard, I looked at the pages of fashion models from *Vogue* and *Harper's Bazaar* scrapbooked across my bedroom walls. For seventeen years, fashion and style had been my life. My first drawings were of stick figures in billowing gowns, jean flares covered in rhinestones, and towering heels. As I got older, fashion became an escape from my average, everyday reality growing up in Allentown, Pennsylvania, where I was homeschooled for twelve years. My parents brought me up on stacks of colorfully illustrated books of saints, videos such as *Jesus of Nazareth*, devotions to Mother Teresa, and the ever-present reminder that all things in life should be oriented toward Christ.

Every Sunday, I would flounce up the steps of my parish church in a kooky vintage dress your eccentric grandma would wear. Faith and style had coexisted in my life since I first learned the Our Father and the Hail Mary. My mother would try to quell my love for material goods by saying, "Catholics should be *in* the world but not *of* the world," a slogan that has been circulating in Catholic circles since medieval times.

My heart raced whenever I paged through glamorous magazine spreads. I wanted to be a part of that world so badly that my insides ached. So, I had to ask, "Does my love for clothing and style make me 'of the world'? Does my passion for self-expression through material things make me materialistic?" The lines between the positives and negatives of the fashion world became blurred. For every thoughtfully crafted ensemble, there was a half-naked woman on a billboard in Times Square. I wondered, *Was fashion completely tainted by sexual objectification? At the core of my desire, was I just seeking attention through my outfits?*

Growing up, I heard that "a good Catholic girl should go to a good Catholic school." I tried looking into the crystal ball of my future. I could see myself at FIT in Manhattan, a montage scene of me catching cabs in slinky silk dresses and partying on roof tops with a martini in hand. It all swirled together: glittering lights, skyscrapers, flashing cameras, models on runways, flowing fabric. It was an idealized reality, one that I could only see Anne Hathaway or Sarah Jessica Parker existing in, not Lilly Fallon. To be honest, it was an environment that I was afraid I would lose myself in, a world in which I could lose my love for God, forever. I didn't feel like I could be both Catholic and a "fashion girl."

So my fears won. Twelve hundred miles later, I stepped off of the plane into the humid haze of southwest Florida. I was a long way from Manhattan, but the excited pit in my stomach told me I was where I was supposed to be.

My first three years at Ave Maria University were a blur of sunshine, palm trees, sandy afternoons on the beach, friendships, hours in Adoration before the Blessed Sacrament, and sleepless nights studying for classes that I didn't naturally excel in. Every summer and Christmas break, I was eager to get back on campus, but not for the academics. I simply wasn't an academic type, and my creative passions felt estranged and useless among classmates who dreamed of Capitol Hill and grad school. My dreams of fashion seemed foolish in comparison, so I moved onto more "practical" dreams, choosing journalism even though it never lit a fire in me. But that was adulthood, right? Doing the "smart" job instead of the one you loved?

I took on journalism internships and headed up the college newspaper as editor-in-chief. Funnily enough, the most well-received article I ever wrote for the paper was about (you guessed it) personal style. The flame was still going strong, even in secret, but I didn't know how it fit into Sacred Scripture 101, metaphysics, or ethics.

THE DAY EVERYTHING CHANGED

Junior year rolled around, and I signed up for the class every upperclassman raved about—Theology of the Body (TOB). This was the class that senior couples took, and many ended up engaged before graduation. The professor, Dr. Michael Waldstein, had a unique expertise in this subject, as he had translated St. John Paul's TOB reflections into English. I slumped into the classroom, wondering, *Why am I taking a class on marriage? I'm not even dating anyone.*

From the classroom window, Dr. Waldstein could be seen merrily riding his bike down the palm-lined sidewalk. Soon, he burst through the door, clad in a traditional Austrian blazer and hands overwhelmed with well-worn books. He strode to his desk, looked around at his new class, and beamed.

Isn't it crazy how, just like that, one person can change your whole life?

When he spoke, every ear listened intently. I don't know if it was his Austrian accent or the passion with which he spoke, but Dr. Waldstein described the human person in a way I had never heard before. The zeal he had for St. John Paul's work was obvious and infectious. I soon realized that the Theology of the Body wasn't just a good Catholic's guide to chastity, sex, and marriage; it was the ultimate anthropology of the human person. It was a lightning rod to the truth of our being, showing where we came from and why we exist.

Hunched over the pages of the Theology of the Body, I read along as Dr. Waldstein quoted St. John Paul II: "The structure of [man's] body is such that it permits him to be the author of genuinely human activity. In this activity, the body expresses the person."[1]

The body expresses the person.

It was as if a million puzzle pieces suddenly clicked into place. Do you know the first thing that popped into my mind when I heard this? *Style.* Sure, it might sound ridiculous that my immediate thought had nothing directly to do with the subject matter, but it was the moment I experienced reconciliation with my deepest passion—which for years had felt like a guilty pleasure.

As Dr. Waldstein further explained St. John Paul II's words, "the body manifests the soul," my brain rearranged itself to make room for the incoming flood of ideas. A thought surfaced, and I scribbled it into the margins of my book: "If the body manifests the soul, then the things we wear can aid this manifestation." I realized that if the nature of the body is so significant in the expression of the human person, the way we dress our bodies must be important, too.

In one class, Dr. Waldstein explained that the Catholic Faith rejects the idea that the materialism of the body is opposed to the soul. On the contrary, he explained that the body and soul are inseparable: "This 'body' reveals the 'living Soul' which Man became when God–Yahweh breathed life into him."[2] The materiality of the body is *good*. Our bodies are not merely fleshy vessels or distractions for getting to heaven. Our bodies *manifest* our souls.

For years, I subconsciously thought that my body restricted my soul and that every time I put together an outfit, I limited myself by drawing attention to the materialism of my body and my clothes. But St. John Paul II reveals that the materiality of the body is necessary for the expression of the soul. One line stood out to me in particular: "The body, in fact, and only the body, is capable of making visible what is invisible: the spiritual and the divine."[3] Again, I couldn't help but see the correlation to personal style. Because the body manifests the soul and the soul is expressed through our bodies, the things we choose to wear can communicate the invisible beauty of the soul while dignifying the visible beauty of the body.

Images exploded before my eyes: outfits of vibrant colors, sumptuous fabrics, and striking silhouettes, all adorning the body, aiding in the expression of the unseen—the soul. I was filled with a desire to pay reverence to my body, to dignify it with the clothing I wore, and to choose items that emphasized the beauty of my soul. We can tangibly see the beauty of shapes, fabric, colors, and textures, but more importantly, the intangible beauty of the human person shines through it all.

Suddenly, my love for the expression of beauty through clothing was no longer silly, materialistic, or unimportant. With the Theology of the Body informing my understanding of the body–soul unity of the person, the significance of personal style became undeniable.

I realized that the things we wear are a visible sign of the relationship between the internal and external, the inseparable unity between body and soul. It felt like I had locked myself in a house for so many years and, finally, doors were being flung open left and right. The power of style wasn't limited to the wearer; it could impact those around us to come to realize their identity as children of God. I thought to myself, "One day, I'm going to write a book about this."

Not only did it feel like I had received permission to embrace style, but I felt like I had been given a mission to share the truths found in the Theology of the Body through personal style. *What if more women understood their true identity as someone made in the image of God? What if style could help them get there?* I thought. The fire that had been burning inside of me since I was a child tripled in size. It all made sense now—both faith *and* style. In fact, style only made sense through the lens of faith. The purpose of clothing doesn't just stop at the practical; rather, it is a tool for evangelization and both personal and spiritual growth.

LIVING MY DREAM

My dream of working in the fashion industry after graduation reemerged. But I was left wondering where I would be able to write about trends while simultaneously explaining the relationship between the body and soul.

During my senior year, I snagged an internship with a small but impactful magazine in New York. It was a dream come true. By graduation, I found myself at the classic Disney Channel movie crossroads. I had to choose between moving to Manhattan to pursue fashion at the magazine or moving to Washington, DC, for a fellowship with *USA Today*. The latter option seemed more practical, and I worried that following dreams was only something movie heroines were allowed to do. When I prayed, however, I was consoled by the peace I felt when discerning a call to the opportunity in New York. With my suitcase full of wacky vintage dresses, I followed that peace all the way to Queens, where I moved in with my aunt and commuted to Manhattan for the next four years.

What began as an internship turned into an editorial assistant position, which then turned into associate style editor, and finally style editor. Being on set at my first photo shoot still goes down as one of the best days of my life. In a giant studio, I was amazed by the beauty of the creative process. What began as a little idea in my mind turned into a reality right before me. The models I scouted were in the clothes I selected and styled, getting their makeup done by the artist I hired, before being captured by a real professional photographer. As the camera flashes went off and the images popped up on the monitor, I couldn't believe my vision was coming to life, just as I had imagined it. I had gone from being the girl who collaged fashion magazine photos on her walls to being the person directing them! It was a high I had never experienced before.

LOST IN THE CROWD

My years at the magazine were full of highs and lows. Following my initial, life-changing encounter with the Theology of the Body, I had to learn many of its lessons firsthand to understand its truth on a personal level. I moved to New York wanting to "be someone" in the fashion industry, and as a result, I became like everyone else. When you picture Manhattan, you probably imagine people stalking the streets in everything from platform boots to feather boas, tutus, and pink leather pants. You might be surprised at how many clones roam its streets.

I will never forget barely making it onto the train heading downtown for work for the first time. It was during the heat of summer, and the smog of the city clung to every passenger. Conspicuously wiping the sweat from my lip, I quickly adjusted my crimson red pencil skirt and striped shirt. I was ready for my debut into the bold New York style scene! But when I looked around the train, everyone was wearing head-to-toe black. Can you believe that movies and television shows can't be trusted for accurate portrayals?

After that first day of work, I aimlessly wandered around the city to soak up as much of the wonder as possible. I observed the women's style and instead of seeing a Carrie Bradshaw on every corner, I saw the same trendy items on everyone. But there was an allure to this sleek Manhattanite woman with her of-the-moment relevancy. The way she traipsed to catch herself a cab, breezy slacks and tunic gently hanging off her frame, designer handbag in the crook of her elbow. She was effortless; she was successful; she was someone who had made it in New York.

Of course, when my first paycheck arrived, I marched myself downtown Broadway to Soho. I plucked my own breezy slacks from store displays and started to fill my wardrobe with neutral, monochrome items. Every day, I was excited to get dressed in the new identity I picked off the racks at Zara. *I'm one step closer to being a Manhattan woman, one step closer to being someone,* I thought. Surely, if I dressed the part, the rest would follow, right?

Not exactly. As the days went by, my trendy outfits felt more like a facade. I had become increasingly insecure in my appearance and in what others thought of me. I didn't feel like the sleek women I saw in Greenwich Village, and I certainly didn't feel like myself anymore. One afternoon, as I was walking home, I caught my reflection in a window. For a few moments, I did not recognize myself. I was indistinguishable in the crowd. I had lost myself.

At that moment, I realized I had forgotten everything I had learned in the Theology of the Body. I wasn't dressing as a woman defined by God but as a woman seeking to be defined by the world. I wanted the approval and affirmation of the fashion industry and the culture around me to show that I was "someone." As I became entrenched in Manhattan culture, I stopped looking at myself through a theological lens. I became obsessed with becoming someone else, not who God had called me to be. The more I conformed to the world, the more I lost my true identity. I sat in shock on the train ride home, wondering what happened to the girl who dressed in vibrant plaids and leopard prints. I wanted to be a girl who knew who she was again.

FAST FASHION WITHDRAWAL

So I made a sudden decision. I quit fashion "cold turkey." I stopped reading magazines, unfollowed bloggers, and, most importantly, stopped shopping trendy fashion. Like a true addict, I went through a period of detox. My brain had become so accustomed to the hits of dopamine I got every time I bought something, I physically felt a longing for the instant gratification of swiping my card and having something new to "improve" myself with.

After two months of shopaholic withdrawal, I didn't feel the urge to buy fast fashion clothes anymore. It was like a veil being lifted from my eyes. I would walk into the old Zara stores that used to call me off the streets with their siren song ("20% off!" they sang) and felt absolutely nothing when I looked through the racks. The rose-colored glasses had come off and I began to see how poorly made the designs actually were—how the fabric was see-through, pilling, or misshapen, and how the construction of the garment had frayed seams, no lining, and raw hems.

For the first time, I also came to appreciate the true state of clothing production. The inhumane working conditions of fashion factories throughout the world was the final straw. So I made the choice to shop exclusively second-hand or from ethical brands. As I became a vintage and thrift store regular, I was exposed to one-of-a-kind, high-quality garments from different decades—at a fraction of the price. Shopping in a thrift store was like a treasure hunt. The excitement of possibility would bubble in my chest as I leafed through hundreds of hangers, "What will I find today?" It was a game of fashion history roulette. Every time I stumbled across the perfect item, it felt like destiny.

THE DIFFERENCE BETWEEN PERSONAL STYLE AND FASHION

It was during this time that I realized just how different personal style and fashion are.

The words "fashion" and "style" are almost always used synonymously, and the muddling of these terms confused my own understanding of the purpose of personal style.

Take a moment to think about the term "fashion." What images come to mind? Now think about "style." What comes to mind? Most people think of "fashion" and imagine the fast-paced New York lifestyle we see in movies and television. We see luxury designer items made for runways, red carpets, editorial spreads, and the upper echelon. Fashion is an elite universe for the rich and famous (or those trying to be). For many of us, though, the word "style" brings to mind women such as Audrey Hepburn, Jane Birken, and Iris Apfel. That's the difference right there. When we think about fashion, we think about an industry. When we think about style, we think of a person. Fashion is the clothes, whereas style is the wearer. Style is and always has been about the expression of the human person. When we confuse the two, we end up losing the significance of personal style and its universality.

While the fashion industry exists for a select few, style is for everyone. A woman who shops at thrift stores can be more stylish than a woman who shops on Fifth Avenue. Style is significant to the individual and has almost nothing to do with the artistic pursuits of fashion designers. Style is internal because it has the power to express visually what we cannot verbally (more on that later). Style has the power to reveal who we are in a way that is unique to ourselves and our clothing. It is an approach, a method, a technique that has been chosen by you to best represent who you are as a person. We can use fashion and designer clothes to express our personal style, but we don't need them.

A great example of the difference between high fashion and style is Audrey Hepburn versus Lady Gaga. Hepburn wasn't cutting edge or over-the-top with her clothes. She wasn't fashionable; she was stylish. She is considered a style icon because her spirit came out in the way she carried herself, spoke, and dressed. It was her style that visually communicated how special she was internally. Thus, we love the woman, not just how she dressed. Many women want to emulate the woman Audrey Hepburn was by adopting some of her most famous outfits.

In contrast, Lady Gaga's extreme fashion choices made her stand out in a different way. In the early years of her fame, we anxiously anticipated her insane ensembles on the red carpet—and she rarely disappointed us. Do you remember her meat dress or when she arrived at the Grammy awards inside of an egg, waiting to hatch? Gaga's fashion has everything to do with the shock and awe of modern art. Her attire usually expressed an overarching message, rather than who she was internally. What she wore wasn't meant to be "liked" but to stun the viewer and convey some meaning.

By misconstruing fashion and style, we lose the meaning, purpose, and significance of both. As Catholics, it is especially important to note the significance of personal style because it is a sign of being made in the image of God.

When I decided to quit pursuing trends, my creativity exploded. Without the influence of trends, I was tapping into my imagination like a kid again. Why couldn't I wear jeans under a dress? Ruffles with camo? Tasseled military coats with leather skirts? Why shouldn't I wear early twentieth-century velvet coats with combat boots? Puffy Austrian dirndl blouses with graphic tees? My inspiration had been turned on like a faucet and it was spilling out all over my wardrobe. Finally, I was wearing what I wanted to—not what an industry told me to.

I flounced through avenues and boulevards, more confident than ever. St. John Paul II's wisdom rang through my ears, "The human being is always unique and unrepeatable, somebody thought of and chosen from eternity, some called and identified by his own name."[4] His words never felt truer to me as I began to express my own identity through personal style. Every bold silhouette, vibrant pattern, or billowing fabric I wore helped me to look in the mirror and realize, "Wow, God *did* make me." The external manifestation of my individuality through style reaffirmed this truth of my unrepeatable identity as a child of God. With every outfit that expressed the unseen beauty of my soul while dignifying my body, I learned to see myself as someone who was so desperately wanted and loved by her Creator.

I began to look at others around me differently. Sitting on the train, I observed my fellow commuters. Laugh-lined faces, slumping postures, phone-scrolling hands, and weary eyes— they too were made in the Image, someone "chosen from eternity ... called and identified by name." While I had spent years recoiling from these people on the cramped train, they were loved by God in ways I could never fathom.

THE BEGINNING OF THE END

Work at the magazine was going great; my Style and Beauty sections had reached their highest viewer count ever. I had developed the identity of those sections to reflect the revelations I had experienced. Every week, I pumped out articles on the significance of style, how the external reveals the internal, and promoted sustainable fashion over fast fashion. During Fashion Week, I would clear my schedule to watch models stomp down runways. When street-style photographers asked to take photos of my outfit after the shows, my heart swelled. In many ways, my life felt like a movie. I spent Saturdays in the East Village perusing my favorite vintage shops, Sunday brunches in the West Village, and Friday nights on the Upper West Side devouring whole pizzas. On especially dreamy nights, I walked along the edge of Central Park listening to Frank Sinatra sing about fairy tales coming true as "Young at Heart" filled my earbuds.

Some late nights, I visited Fifth Avenue to watch the designers change the window displays at Saks and Bergdorf Goodman for the new season. During Christmastime, I would sip on Godiva hot chocolate and look up at the lights that canopied the streets. I relished being consumed by it all.

Just after Christmas of 2017, I was let go from my job. So, just like that, almost four years of "living the dream" was over.

I entered a two-year period of crisis, desperately grasping onto the identity I had built for myself upon skyscrapers, VIP treatment from brands, my "style editor" title, and everything that came with being "someone" in New York. I spent my first year trying to escape my new reality by traveling around the country and, finally, jet-setting to Europe on a one-way ticket. *Maybe I won't go back,* I thought. If I was the cool, "wanderlust" girl, that would make up for being unemployed, right? Three weeks later, I was back in Pennsylvania. Apparently, wanderlust doesn't work when you are broke.

Moving out of New York was like being kicked out of an apartment. As a teenager, I had plastered maps of Manhattan all over my bedroom walls, but now I watched its skyline fading into the horizon as the Greyhound bus drove me away. I had given back the keys to the world's greatest city, and I wasn't sure if I would ever be welcomed back again. Hauling my things to the third floor of my parents' house in Pennsylvania, I was a kid waiting for her life to begin all over again. I tried to support myself by diving into freelance writing, but it was never enough. I applied to endless fashion-related jobs in the city, but I never heard back from any of them.

In anger, I prayed to the Lord, "How could you do this to me?" I spent months in oversized sweats and my hair in greasy, messy buns in my childhood bedroom. On Friday nights, I drove my parents' car to Walmart to buy frozen pizzas and rent videos from Redbox. I looked out at the parking lot full of "average," "normal" people. I was one of them now. I no longer felt special because of my job or where I lived. I was stripped of the identity I had taken pride in, and I had nothing left except for an Instagram grid full of photos from my past life.

LIFTING THE VEIL

Several months later, I found myself on a Greyhound back to Manhattan for Fashion Week. This time, though, I was assisting my favorite designer label with their show. I told myself, *This is going to be my big break!* It was my re-entry into the life I deserved. Surely, God wouldn't arbitrarily bless me with my dream gig if he didn't want this for my future. When I arrived at the studio, I marveled at the designer garments hanging on industrial clothing racks in a room with floor-to-ceiling windows. They were pieces I had seen in editorial spreads, on the runway, and on red carpets. I was thrown into a week-long tizzy of dressing and undressing models, running last-minute, late-night errands to the seamstress, and my least favorite task—getting coffee and lunch for everyone.

But it was all worth it to watch the label's stylist place her finger on her lip, tilt her head, and wave her hand like a wand toward the items she wanted styled together. She mixed and matched pieces no one would have thought of—short skirts on top of dresses, dresses on top of dresses, tall boots with midi-length skirts, long jackets over short dresses. Her choices were entirely unconventional yet intricately beautiful. She handed me her new creations all day, "Have the model try these together." I would help the model slip into these strange garment formulas, and she would emerge from the dressing room to show the designers her walk. They carefully eyed her every step, determining whether this look would end up in the show. Once they all agreed, they took a photograph of the look so we could pin it to the final-look board later.

Every day was nonstop. The night before the show, we were at the studio until three a.m., zipping up garment bags in the order of the model lineup, tagging them, updating information on the computer, and waiting for last-minute additions to be completed by the seamstresses who zoomed away at their sewing machines. The designers were long gone; it was just the team working into the morning, our seven a.m. wake-up call looming.

When my alarm went off, I bolted out of bed, got dressed, snagged my "VIP Fashion Week" lanyard off the hook, and ran to catch the train. When I arrived at the show location, our models sat in a line of folding chairs as makeup and hair artists feverishly buzzed around them. It was exactly like the behind-the-scenes fashion show blogs I had consumed as a kid. The showrunner yelled for the models to line up for a test walk in their shoes, and when they came back, it was a frenzy of getting them dressed in their "looks." When they were all ready, they waited in the lineup as a hoard of backstage photographers snapped away.

When the music started, it was "go-time." One by one, the models filed out of the backstage area and onto the runway. We watched eagerly as the garments we had handled for the previous seven days were photographed for the pages of *Vogue* and *Harper's Bazaar*. And then, just like that, it was all over. We had spent hours preparing for a show that was done in seven minutes. The models came back, took off their looks, and left. We carefully zipped the items back into their garment bags, and the designers waved before leaving, saying, "Hey, thanks for helping! See you next time." And there was a next time, a few more, actually. I found myself assisting whenever they had a photo shoot, sample sale, or runway show. In the beginning, I prayed for a full-time position, but I started to feel the veil being lifted once again.

It began when I was asked to Uber to a salad shop across town because the one we were all ordering from didn't have the croutons the stylist wanted. Then I needed to retrieve the designer's lost ID at a bar after he had been partying a bit too hard the night before. My eyes were opened to the way industry professionals treated people "below them."

During a sample sale, I was hired to organize garments for certain wealthy women of Manhattan. They poured through the doors, designer bags in tow, filler in their lips, not a wrinkle in sight, grabbing $3,000 dresses like it was BOGO day at Walmart. They stripped down to their La Perla underwear in the middle of the studio, talking about vacations in Greece, weddings in Sicily, weekends in the Hamptons as I zipped and buttoned. "What a great deal!!" one exclaimed, as she zipped her credit card through the iPhone card reader to pay the amount of $12,000.

I felt like Alice falling through the rabbit hole into a parallel reality where it was foolish not to buy the neon pink jacket. I observed the upper echelon teeter off in their stilettos with their new purchases, back to their penthouses high in the sky. No matter how many magazines and fashion movies I gobbled up as a kid, it was only then that I saw the fashion world for what it was—an industry that existed to perpetuate itself, season after season, in the hopes of remaining relevant. But relevant for whom? For what?

When the designers said to me, "See you next time!" I was thrown onto the conveyor belt, becoming an eyewitness to the endless cycle of producing expensive clothes for the rich and famous. Conversations revolved around their appearance, their vacations, and what famous people they could boast about knowing. Like a fly on the wall, I absorbed it all. It was an exclusive universe completely disconnected from ninety-nine percent of the world. It seemed to be governed by extremely thin, blonde, white women. I stuck out like a sore thumb. Where were *ordinary* woman in this elitist world?

The final straw was when I was asked to babysit the designer's child during a major photo shoot that I had spent a week helping prepare for. At the playground, the photo shoot coordinator texted me, "Where are you?!? You're missing everything!" As I walked back after stopping for ice cream, I suddenly realized I *wanted* to miss everything that had to do with fashion. After spending my whole life pining to be a part of this industry, I wanted nothing to do with it.

A NEW MISSION

That bus ride home was different this time. I didn't want to go back to Manhattan. I didn't want to be the fashion girl I had dreamed of becoming anymore. In a bittersweet mix of emotions, I felt bereft of my identity and released from its chains at the same time. For the first time in my life, I had no idea what I wanted to be "when I grew up." I waited for the fashion itch to come back, but it never did. I kept checking within myself the same way you repeatedly check the fridge for food, aimlessly opening the door and expecting food to appear.

It was clear that God had led me to that gig on purpose—to reveal that the fashion industry was not what I had idealized it to be. I had thought failure was the worst-case scenario for lost dreams. But what if I simply didn't want the dream anymore? Since our culture defines a person's success by the dreams he or she pursues and achieves, losing that direction left me feeling ashamed and purposeless.

"God, what do you want for me? Do you want *anything* for me?" I desperately prayed. I was struggling to keep up with my bills as a freelance writer, and I was embarrassed to be living at home with no goal or passion in life. Overwhelmed with anxiety, I went to church and looked up at the crucifix hanging over the altar. With my last straw of sanity, I prayed for direction, for any semblance of guidance. In the silence, a clear thought popped into my head: "You're a writer. So write."

Peace came over me like a warm bucket of water being poured over my head. The first thing I thought of was a book. In truth, the flame that had been burning in me for fashion as a kid was like that of a small candle. But when I was introduced to the Theology of the Body in college, it was stoked into a blazing torch. Though this flame had been dampened by my worldly pursuits, in the back of my mind a voice prodded me to write about the Theology of the Body and personal style.

That day, I went home rejuvenated and confident in the path to which God was calling me. For months I had been filled with anxiety, doubt, and confusion, which had left me depressed and sullen. But now, all of this was lifted. I thought maybe it was a temporary high and that those feelings would come back in a few weeks, but they never did. I was more certain of this calling than anything else in my life.

So I decided it was time to start writing. It made sense to call this book *Theology of Style*. I got to work, diving back into St. John Paul II all over again. I combed through his words, discovering pages of wisdom that related to the expression of the human person through style. I began writing about personal style through a theological lens for different Catholic publications and on Instagram. Women began responding positively, telling me they related to my story or that I had put words to their own thoughts on femininity, style, fashion, and the human body. I waded into topics about the willful separation of body and soul, materialism, the objectification of the body, the evangelizing power of beauty, and the gift of creativity and divine collaboration.

I began speaking on podcasts and live streams, and I gave talks to different small groups, classes, and conferences. This book has been the ultimate goal of this mission, and it has been a long journey of feeling nervous and overwhelmed by the task. I asked myself if I was qualified or skilled enough, but every time I was faced with internal opposition, I was filled with reassurance through the passion I felt whenever I started writing.

As you dive into the rest of this book, here is a guiding message to take with you: Personal style is merely a tool for better understanding how and why you were made. Ironically, personal style has nothing to do with being "stylish" or relevant in the world. Rather, it is a tangible expression of the relationship between the body and soul, a visible sign of being made in the image of God. Style is a reminder of your inherent worth in the eyes of the Creator—a worth that is unchanging, regardless of what you are wearing. This book isn't primarily about personal style but the truths revealed in the Theology of the Body and the power they have to completely change your life.

Part 2

THEOLOGY OF STYLE

IS STYLE AN ART?

*A*s we dive into what Theology of Style is, we should ask ourselves: "Would St. John Paul II approve of this concept?" We are, after all, viewing style through the lens of his work.

You might recall a particularly cool black-and-white photo of Karol Wojtyla as a young priest, wearing a pair of Ray-Ban shades and a beret. Yes, the man had style. The future pope was no stranger to artistic expression, as his youth was full of poetry, playwriting, and acting. Can you believe that prior to being ordained, he co-founded a theater company and almost pursued a career in the business? Staying true to his roots even during his pontificate, he performed his poetry for a video cassette published by the Vatican in 1999! In the same year, he wrote his *Letter to Artists*, which has become a beloved manifesto. This document serves as a bridge between the artist and the Church, strengthening the relationship by validating the vocation of the artist by defining art's true source and purpose. To study any theological significance that style might have, we must explore St. John Paul II's definition of art and the role of the artist. Our question is: Can style be considered an art form?

St. John Paul II opens his *Letter to Artists* by stating, "None can sense more deeply than you artists, ingenious creators of beauty that you are, something of the pathos with which God at the dawn of creation looked upon the work of his hands."[5] So right off the bat, he describes artists as creators of beauty, mirroring the creative power of God himself. He continues, "Captivated by the hidden power of sounds and words, colours and shapes, you have admired the work of your inspiration, sensing in it some echo of the mystery of creation with which God, the sole creator of all things, has wished in some way to associate you."[6] St. John Paul II immediately confirms the significance and identity of the artist, describing him as someone who has been chosen by the Creator. Someone who is akin to God through the ability to reveal divine beauty. This is an important gift, and John Paul II is very clear that it is the job of artists to create art that is beautiful and worthwhile so that they may enrich their cultural heritage while also serving the common good. In short, it is a gift from God to be used for the greater good of mankind. We could also describe it as a mission.

The question we are led to, then, is this: What makes art, *art*? What are the criteria for being considered true art, worthy of God's association? According to St. John Paul II, "Art must make perceptible, and as far as possible attractive, the world of the spirit, of the invisible, of God."[7] Essentially, true art makes visible the divine. True art reveals God. He goes on to explain, "The link between good and beautiful stirs fruitful reflection." In other words, art should lead man to contemplate the Author of beauty and lift his senses to the eternal. Many of us have experienced this in our own lives, probably multiple times.

Take a moment to consider a time you were absolutely moved by beauty. Perhaps you walked into a cathedral with vaulted ceilings that seemed to reach into heaven itself, listened to Debussy's haunting "Clair de lune," or wandered through the Metropolitan Museum of Art and came across *Joan of Arc* by Jules Bastien-Lepage. Recall a moment in which you were completely enraptured yet at peace, allowing time to stand still as your heart and mind were taken by the beauty before you. Where did your mind go during that moment? What questions did you ask yourself?

I will never forget standing on top of a mountain in Sedona, Arizona, rusty colored clay crunching beneath my feet. Looking out at the red rocks stretching for miles and up into the sky, the question that popped into my head was, "Who is responsible for this?" I was suddenly aware of my smallness in the magnificence of it all—so small compared to the mind of this landscape's maker. Even though I was looking out at a beautiful scene, I felt like I was looking at God.

True art has this same effect. Our culture is full of incredible works that have brought men and women to their knees, marveling at the beauty of God even though their eyes behold the ceiling of the Sistine Chapel, for example. Art's transcendental nature reaches into the core of our being, prompting existential questions like, "How is man able to create such beauty? What is the source of beauty?" Which then leads to, "Who made me?" And in our smallness, humbled yet lifted up by our encounter with something greater than ourselves, we may even venture to ask, "Why am I here? What is my purpose?"

True art points the viewer to the Creator of the universe. As St. John Paul II writes, "Every genuine art form in its own way is a path to the inmost reality of man and of the world."[8] This is why he was so passionate about the significance of the role of artists, because he believed that beauty was the vocation of the artist, a special gift. He implies that beauty is a "team effort" in which God invites artists to be his disciples, spreading truth through the talent he has bestowed upon them. Beauty through art is a collaborative effort by mankind and God to give souls a glimpse of the divine.

Art is a two-sided coin, however. At the same time art's ultimate purpose is to reveal the Creator, it also reveals a great deal of who the artist is. St. John Paul II says, "In producing a work, artists express themselves to the point where their work becomes a unique disclosure of their own being, of what they are and of how they are ... In shaping a masterpiece, the artist not only summons his work into being, but also in some way reveals his own personality by means of it."[9] This makes sense. Consider, for example, the internal turbulence present within each stroke of a Vincent van Gogh painting. In viewing his work, we can witness elements of his passion, his struggles, his isolation, and his whimsical nature. This is especially true with his self-portraits, where his emotion is practically jumping off the canvas. We see who Van Gogh is in an honest, open, and real way. We are moved by who he is. Art reveals God's creation, which includes us, his children. In exposing the innermost depths of our being through our art, it points back to the Being who created us— God himself.

Mankind is a part of God's creation, and the beauty of the human person similarly points toward the source of it all. Mankind is God's most beloved creation, made in his image and likeness, with both body and soul. In our very being, we carry his likeness. Not every person, of course, makes an effort to actively express who God is and not all art points back toward the Creator; sometimes it stops at the artist or even at the artist's brokenness. St. John Paul II explains: "Art has a unique capacity to take one or other facet of the message and translate it into colours, shapes and sounds which nourish the intuition of those who look or listen. It does so without emptying the message itself of its transcendent value and its aura of mystery."[10] When he says "message," he means the beauty that leads to truth and goodness.

So, who are these artists? How do we know if we have been called to this artistic vocation? Throughout his *Letter to Artists*, John Paul refers to painters, sculptors, musicians, and the like, but his parting words include more diverse professions, "I appeal to you, artists of the written and spoken word, of the theatre and music, of the plastic arts and the most recent technologies in the field of communication."[11] If he included more modern examples of art, we can guess at his openness to personal style, especially in that he references communication (as style is a way of communicating and expressing).

In the dedication of his letter, St. John Paul II describes artists as "those who are passionately dedicated to the search for new 'epiphanies' of beauty so that through their creative work as artists they may offer these as gifts to the world." In a world full of dancers, architects, filmmakers, seamstresses, muralists, and photographers, the title of artist cannot solely belong to those of more typical roles like painter and sculptor because the gift of beauty can be created and given through many diverse methods. But when asked to list different modes of artistic expression, most people wouldn't put personal style at the top of the list. So how would we compare the obvious examples of art with the not-so-obvious?

Perhaps we think of painters, sculptors, and writers as artists first because the product of their talent and work is tangible. Their art is physically "outside" of them. But what about art that isn't technically "outside" of the artist? For example, take actors, singers, and dancers. They create art, but this art is not an object to be held in one's hands or seen in a museum. They express their art through their very own physical form. It is a part of their bodies. This medium of art is closely tied with the physical nature of the person who is creating it. The argument for art expressed via clothing lies in the middle ground between tangible and intangible art. This art exists somewhere between the painter and the dancer, combining elements of the tangible (i.e., physical clothes that express material beauty) and the intangible (i.e., the beauty that comes from the internal expression of the human person). If you have clothes on a mannequin or on a hanger, this is like musical notes on a page. There is a sense in which it is art, but in a way that lacks a crucial animus. Clothing on a person is like those notes being played out; it is the "same" art, but consummate and animated.

Again, St. John Paul's words come into play: "Art has a unique capacity to take one or other facet of the message and translate it into colours, shapes and sounds which nourish the intuition of those who look or listen." When it comes to the things we wear, we can tangibly see the beauty of shapes, fabric, colors, textures, but more importantly it emphasizes the intangible beauty of the human person. Think of a time when you were taken aback by the beauty of someone's ensemble. Maybe you were taken by a classic like Grace Kelly's blue chiffon dress from *To Catch a Thief* or Audrey Hepburn's entire wardrobe in *Funny Face*. Or perhaps you are drawn to modern-day moments of genius, like Jenna Lyons' print mixing masterpieces from J. Crew. Or perhaps you can recall a time when your mom, sister, aunt, or friend wore something that communicated a deeper beauty that reflects who she is as a person.

Just the other day, my friend Kathleen wore a deep blue striped dress with a belt that cinched it in at the waist and a pair of woven sandals. I see her every day, but at that moment I was on the outside looking in. Everything about her seemed to radiate, what she wore just emphasized her beauty as a whole person. Interior qualities and traits that make Kathleen unique and wonderful were being expressed through how she dressed that day. Looking at her I thought, "Wow, my friend really is a beautiful person." Haven't we all experienced moments like this?

When an outfit especially highlights someone's identity, making you take a step back to appreciate everything they are? Maybe in those moments, you even thank God for creating this person who you cherish so dearly.

These sartorial moments have the power of revealing the unseen; making tangible the intangible beauty of the human person who reflects the perfect beauty of the Creator. This can lead us to contemplate the Being that brought this person into existence. Encountering the beauty of the human person in the flesh, I would argue, is even more powerful than the greatest work of art. For Christ dwells within each of us, and it is in every good trait we possess that we mirror his goodness. St. John Paul II said that true art makes visible the beauty of God. Through his criteria, it seems foolish to discount the significance of clothing, which reaches beyond mere pieces of fabric.

You might be thinking, "Well, I've seen a lot of outfits that don't exactly reflect beauty." That's true. Just as we can choose to express our inherent beauty through how we dress, we can also detract from it. The way we dress can be emptied of its purpose for communicating the human person and by extension, the Creator. Sometimes we wear revealing clothing, follow trends manufactured for the masses, or simply don't care about what we wear. This is why so many disregard the artistic power of clothing. Many choose not to celebrate their inherent beauty, and some are misguided by the culture. While clothing can be a powerful expression of beauty, it can also be the opposite. Sometimes the things we wear do not offer an encounter with our whole person, but only superficial parts or manifestations of our fractured identity.

The reason we don't commonly associate the way we dress with art is because we have grown accustomed to a culture that frequently reduces or even denies the transcendent value of the human person. This, of course, affects the way we dress. The pursuit of dressing well has become closely tied with a society that prioritizes social status over genuine self-expression and dressing for sexual attention rather than to dignify one's body. As a culture, we have lost the knowledge of being made in the image of God and the full depth of our worth. Because of this, the pursuit of artistic expression through clothing is often reduced to materialistic, vain, worldly, or simply meaningless.

St. John Paul II warned against emptying art of its "transcendent value."[12] I am sure we can all recall a time we encountered art that did not exactly uplift our senses. There can still be power and influence in these types of art, expressing subjective emotion or a message that reflects the struggles of that time. Art reflects the culture and society's relationship with God. Consider most popular songs today. They describe shallow relationships reduced to sex or accumulating excess wealth and status to substitute real meaning. Just because some artistic expressions are "emptied [of] their transcendental value" does not mean that true art within a particular medium cannot exist.

Similarly, simply because the art of dressing has been lost or abused, this does not mean seeking to revive style is an unworthy endeavor, incapable of greatly impacting the individual, society, and culture. The current abuses against personal style should not prevent us from restoring this artistic medium to its intended standard of communicating beauty, truth, and goodness of the human person. If anything, dressing in a way that degrades one's dignity is merely a visible sign of an internal wound that desperately needs healing. We are oriented toward finding a greater meaning and anything that reduces our worth just proves we were made for more. A lack of good simply points toward the good that is intended.

As St. John Paul II writes even further on this point, "Even in situations where culture and the Church are far apart, art remains a kind of bridge to religious experience ... even when they explore the darkest depths of the soul or the most unsettling aspects of evil, artists give voice in a way to the universal desire for redemption."[13] Even if those forms of art have been emptied of transcendental value, it is a sign of what is so painfully lacking in that artist's life and the loss of an identity found in God.

PSYCHOLOGY OF STYLE

Communication is a major element of art. It has the power to communicate who God is as well as who the human person is. Reiterating St. John Paul II's words once more, "Artists express themselves to the point where their work becomes a unique disclosure of their own being ... the artist ... reveals his own personality by means of it."[14] Again, if painting, sculpting, singing, etc., are means for disclosing one's personality, it seems fair to also recognize personal style, a medium famous for self-expression. A medium that uniquely combines the expression of the self through artistic creativity *and* the human form at the same time.

You might still be thinking, "But they're just clothes. Do they really matter? Isn't it better not to care at all about what you look like?" These are good questions. Let's consider body expressions—smiles, tears, and laughter. Do they matter? Of course! What would human interaction be without bodily manifestations of our feelings, emotions, or our soul? Physical expressions flow from our interior life, revealing our deepest feelings, thoughts, and personalities. A laugh expresses one of purest human experiences—joy. Tears show the depths of human suffering. And a smile has a way of revealing our most honest, childlike selves. These expressions are so powerful because they manifest the soul, making visible the invisible.

Our deepest feelings and emotions are manifested through the body, making up our personality, character quirks, and unique mannerisms, informing the world who we are and how God created us. These are expressions of the soul materialized in the body, communicating our very humanity. It is the materiality of the body that expresses the essence of our being to those around us, non-verbally communicating who we are on a micro-level as individuals but also on a macro-level as beings created in the image of God. The physical nature of the body is necessary for this communication. But let's ask ourselves: Wouldn't the material things we choose to put on our bodies also be a part of this physical expression? To what extent do our clothes express and affect our internal identity?

For most, clothing is purely practical. It is something we put on to not be naked, to keep warm or cool, and to look appropriate for specific occasions. Clothing, however, is undeniably very personal. Think about it; clothing rests upon our bodies, it moves with us, goes where we go. It is a part of our appearance and the perception of who we are to ourselves and others. Every day, we choose certain clothes that become a part of our physical appearance, accompanying our bodies in every aspect of life.

As nineteenth-century Scottish historian and philosopher Thomas Carlyle writes in *Sartor Resartus*, "Neither in tailoring nor in legislating does man proceed by mere Accident, but the hand is ever guided on by mysterious operations of the mind. In all his Modes, and habilatory endeavors, an Architectural Idea will be found lurking; his Body and the Cloth are the site and materials wherein and whereby his beautiful edifice, of a Person, is to be built."[15]

In short, the body and the clothing we put on it are where man expresses or "builds" his identity. The act of curating one's sartorial identity is a process in which the individual chooses items that they believe best reflect and express their taste, who they are, what they do for a living, where they live, and how they want to be perceived. Whether we realize it or not, our clothing choices express a vast array of information—what inspires us, our moods, our self-esteem, and who we want to be. It is a method of communication; a way of speaking without saying a single word.

St. John Paul II teaches that the body manifests the soul, working from the account of man's creation in Genesis: "This 'body' reveals the 'living Soul' which Man became when God-Yahweh breathed life into him"[16] (Genesis 2:7). The famous fashion stylist Rachel Zoe echoes this truth, "Style is a way to say who you are without having to speak."[17] Although these thoughts are from two very different people, both of their messages concern the non-verbal language of the human person through the physical.

Consider your own friends and the way they express themselves through their bodies, mannerisms, and facial expressions. Now, think of how they similarly express themselves through the way they dress. Gregarious, bubbly friends might choose to wear bright colors, bold prints. Athletic, active friends might choose to wear comfortable items that allow them to move freely. Eclectic, quirky friends might experiment with mixing patterns, wearing vintage clothes, or unique patterns. Poised and professional friends might stick to classic items. The materiality of our clothes is a part of the material expression of the body. Style, like the body, communicates through a non-verbal language, telling the story of who we are and where we came from. When we meet someone, we learn parts of who they are before they even speak.

Imagine a woman approaching you decked out in layers of jewelry, bright colors, and whimsical fabrics. What information are you able to gather from her self-expression? Perhaps that she likes to have fun with how she expresses herself, that she isn't afraid of standing out, being bold, seen by others, or even being judged. Similarly, imagine meeting someone in head-to-toe gothwear, complete with chains, leather, and black lipstick. Her appearance communicates that she is not afraid to be countercultural yet is seeking a way to fit in with a community. In the end, style is a language we all speak—even if we are not trying to be "stylish." What we wear is very much a part of our personal and social identity. Our clothes are like physical attributes that allow others to recognize our identity. Of course, on a purely practical and social level, our bodies cannot be without clothes, and our clothes have the power to become a feature of our physical identity.

CLOTHING, AN EXTENSION OF THE BODY

This is a concept that has been explored by philosophers, psychologists, and authors for centuries, and it is something we live out every day. For example, when I once wore contacts, my eight-year-old nephew made a face, saying, "You look so different without glasses." I said, "Oh, don't you like it?" He replied, "No, you look different. I like you with glasses." He had become so accustomed to my appearance with glasses that something about who I was seemed altered without them. To him, my glasses were a part of my identity, as something that expressed a defining part of who I was as a person—even though they were just an object and not a true part of my body.

This is an instance of a person's ability to express themselves through an object. The theory of clothing becoming a "part" of the body is something the nineteenth-century German philosopher Hermann Lotze describes in his book *Microcosmus*. He said that any time we bring an object "into relationship with the surface of our body" we invest that object with "the consciousness of our personal existence" taking its shape to be our own and making it part of the self.[18]

Lotze is arguing that the clothes we wear can feel like an extension of our body, that they are an expansion of the "self." As an example, he describes the feeling of wearing hats and shoes: "Once a man has positioned his hat, slightly tilted, atop his head, it is transformed, no longer a lifeless scrap of cloth: Thus arises the pleasing delusion that we ourselves, our own life, and our strength reach up to that point, and at every step that shakes it, at every puff of wind that sets it in motion, we have quite distinctly the feeling as if a part of our own being were solemnly nodding backwards and forwards."[19] His point is that items we wear can make us feel as though we *are* tall, as if our very being has been extended. Similarly, the swaying of garments gives us the sensation of swaying ourselves.

Recall a time when a spring maxi dress made you feel like you were light, delicate, and breezy. The characteristics of the dress seemed to seep into your very soul. There was a transfer of traits that made you feel at one with this item of clothing. The construction, fabric, weight, and embellishments of a garment can impact the interior state of the wearer: "The greater or less tension and firmness possessed by the material in itself, or due to its cut, is transferred to us as if it resulted from our bearing."[20] A woman who chooses to wear beautiful, light, drapey items does not only wear them to dazzle those around her, but "the wearer herself is by feeling directly present in all the graceful curves that with featherweight touch but a few points of the skin, and yet through these points excite the most distinct sensation of the breadth, lightness, and softness of their sweep."[21]

Have you ever experienced this yourself? Reflect on a time your clothes impacted how you felt about yourself. Have you ever worn a dress that transformed how you saw yourself? As you slipped it over your head and fastened the zipper, did it fill you with confidence or help you realize that you truly *are* a beautiful woman? Or have you ever had a challenging day ahead of you and decided to wear your sharpest blazer, confident it would give you the strength you needed? Or worn a pair of shoes that made you walk with a purpose? Or perhaps on a chilly fall day you said, "I want to be cozy," and as you pulled on a pair of sweats and a hoodie, you were indeed "cozy." Clothing can be felt as something that is a part of our bodies, as if the fabric is an extension of our flesh, while also impacting our attitude and self-perception.

William James, the father of American psychology, also writes on the science of dress: "The body is the innermost part of the material self in each of us; certain parts of the body seem more intimately ours than the rest. The clothes come next ... The old saying that the human person is composed of three parts—soul, body and clothes—is more than a joke."[22] How amazing is it that James, a major figure in the history of psychology, is touching on the heart of our study on the relationship between the soul, body, and clothes?

Ironically enough, James' equally famous brother, author Henry James, considers the same topic in *Portrait of a Lady* through the character of Madame Merle. As Merle exclaims, "What shall we call our 'self'? Where does it begin? Where does it end? It overflows into everything that belongs to us—and then it flows back again. I know a large part of myself is in the clothes I choose to wear. I've a great respect for things! One's self—or other people—is one's expression of one's self; and one's house, one's furniture, one's garments, the books one reads, the company one keeps—these things are all expressive."[23]

CLOTHED, BY CHOICE

If the things we wear can be a means for communication, regardless of our intentionality in doing so, then imagine how powerful it is when we deliberately *choose* to communicate ourselves through our dress. With the revelation of the soul through the body, we have a limited say in how those traits are expressed. We can't choose our noses, mouths, natural hair color, or body type. For example, I am 5'10", and I have brown hair and gangly limbs. People can identify me by these inherited features. But people also identify me by the leather coat I always wear, my vintage Levi's jeans, the tortoiseshell glasses that rarely leave my face, and my fingers full of rings. Who I am as Lillian Fallon isn't just the organic stuff, but also the items I choose to express who I am. Sometimes my friends or family members will send me a picture of someone who dresses similarly, saying, "Wow, this looks just like you!" or they will shoot me a message and say, "I wore an oversized blazer today and thought of you." My good friend Michaela once did a style challenge on her Instagram and dressed as all of her stylish friends. Every one of us had recognizable, distinct looks that spoke to the identity of each person.

You might be saying, "Sure, but you're interested in fashion and specifically choose stylish items. Your point doesn't really apply to the everyday person who is not interested in style." To respond, I would argue that we all choose items that express who we are—whether we realize it or not. Nobody is completely indifferent in how they appear to others. Just consider the people around you, your friends, family, co-workers, and classmates. They might not have a particular interest or passion for fashion, but they certainly are not wearing the white and grey unisex clothes seen in futuristic, post-apocalypse films. Rather than being purely utilitarian, there is the element of personal choice in their clothing selection.

Think of the last time you went clothing shopping. When you went into the store, you didn't just randomly buy clothes. No, we gravitate toward items we like, and we are repelled by ones we don't. We subconsciously choose items we feel best represent and reflect who we are, who we want to be, and how we want the world to see us. Even someone who doesn't necessarily have a passion for creative expression or doesn't even care about having "style" will choose something they like. Nobody buys and puts something on their bodies that they positively dislike.

Consider the universal dressing room experience. As you try on your selection of clothes, you start adding to your "no" and "yes" piles. When you slip on something that fits just right, there is a "click." Not only does it fit well, but the color is your favorite, and the pattern seems unique and beautiful to you. As you turn side to side in the mirror, checking yourself from all angles, you smile. You realize that this item truly suits you. It is like it was made for you. Your friend might even say when you emerge from the dressing room, "That's so *you!*"

In this magical moment, there is an alignment between your internal identity and this external garment you just happened across. Even though it is an inanimate object that you found on a clothing rack, it has the power to reflect who you are. We do not simply wear items we are forced to; we choose to wear things with which we identify. This is a personal choice that reflects the intimate nature of creating our own style.

There are people, of course, who especially enjoy and invest in the creative process of choosing items that they feel best reflects their identity. Some are more attuned to their creativity and feel passionately about sharing that through their dress. They might be more naturally aware of the relationship between what we wear and who we are and might make a more conscious effort to intentionally create art through their clothes. They might express this through creating beautifully dramatic silhouettes, bright colors and prints, sumptuous fabrics and textiles, and the blending of different decades in fashion history. More than anything, the clothing we wear is an opportunity to express and know the beauty of our whole person.

POSITIVE REAFFIRMATION OF ONE'S TRUE IDENTITY

Herman Lotze gets even closer to the heart of our study of a "theology of style" by addressing the relationship between clothing and the human soul: "We speak of dress ... our inquiry is exclusively as to the source of the pleasure which they and other kinds of decoration afford to the human soul. It lies by no means only in the gratification of the vanity that seeks to be admired by others, but in the heightened and ennobled vital feeling of the wearer himself."[24] His account touches on my initial concern as a teenager, wondering whether my passion for style was pure vanity. Lotze argues that the way we dress isn't superficial, but an expression of the soul which can positively impact the psychological state of the wearer. We see here again how the internal is manifested through the external, but we are also introduced to the positive effect the external can have on the internal. As Henry James so eloquently points out in *The Portrait of a Lady*, our internal state can impact our exterior expression, our exterior can equally influence our mood, emotions, and confidence.

Incredibly, these reflections on the power of dress came from men in the 1800s! Far from being purely a modern study, the psychology of style and the identity of the human person through their clothes is something great minds have pondered for centuries. It makes sense, however, that the influence of clothing would be explored by psychologists and philosophers because it's so closely associated with the mind. We can wield the power of the way we dress to positively impact our mental state. Personal style is a tool that can be used to positively impact self-esteem and even performance.

This is not unlike positive self-talk. Self-talk is that inner dialogue in our minds, essentially how we speak to ourselves. If you happen to be a woman in today's culture, you are probably familiar with how hard it is to stop negative self-talk when you are looking in the mirror or scrolling through social media. Sometimes we say mean, hurtful things about ourselves, saying we are ugly, worthless, not good enough, or failures. Sometimes we play these nasty comments on a loop, causing us to view ourselves in an extremely negative light. Studies have shown that negative self-talk can greatly impact our self-perception and behavior. Times when we scold or demean ourselves have a visceral effect, causing our confidence to plummet and our concept of self-worth to become skewed.

On the flip side, positive self-talk can do just the opposite by building up our confidence. Studies have shown that positive self-talk improves relationships, increases resilience, reduces stress, and helps construct a healthier perception of oneself. Saying to yourself, "You are loved. You are good enough. You are important," even when you feel the opposite at that moment, can shift the way you see yourself in the long term. Positive self-talk drastically changes your own narrative and corrects your internal dialogue, allowing you to see yourself in a more charitable, truer light.

Of course, speaking kindly to yourself takes a lot of work and consistency to have an impact. In the beginning, this might feel unnatural or inauthentic, but over time it will become a transformative habit. This approach is not unlike growing in prayer, which also requires effort, commitment, and dedication, especially at first. In the beginning, prayer sometimes just feels like words strung together. We might not even want to pray or necessarily be emotionally moved to do so, but we recite the words because we know it's good for us. As time goes on, our prayers transform from one-sided conversations to intimate encounters with God himself. Soon, prayer is no longer a chore but something we look forward to because it helps us to grow in trust and peace, which impacts every aspect of our lives.

I bring up the psychological benefits of positive self-talk and prayer because the way we dress can have a similar effect. Even if you are struggling with self-esteem, self-worth, and confidence, dressing to convey the unique beauty of your soul and the dignity of your body will help you to start seeing yourself as precious and dignified. In the beginning of dressing to express your worth, you might not feel particularly convinced of it. But the more you consistently communicate to yourself that you are a person of infinite value, the more you restore that healthy perception of your true identity as a child of God. This process takes some time, but when you commit to building the habit of honoring your body and soul, you will grow in the knowledge of your inherent worth (something we will dive into more in Part 3).

In his *Letter to Artists*, St. John Paul II states, "The Church has always appealed to [artists'] creative powers in interpreting the Gospel message and discerning its precise application in the life of the Christian community. This partnership has been a source of mutual spiritual enrichment. Ultimately, it has been a great boon for an understanding of man, of the authentic image and truth of the person."[25] In other words, art helps man to have a better understanding of himself, who is made in God's image. This is also true for the way you dress because it can help you recognize your identity as a whole person. How we dress impacts how we see ourselves, allowing us to see ourselves in a truer light—that is, in the light of our creation.

For example, has an outfit ever helped you to recognize how beautiful you truly are? Or has a beautiful dress or super sharp blazer made you realize the dignity of your body and the reverence that is owed to it? Our clothes can reaffirm the beauty of our body–soul unity and the wholeness of our being.

To reiterate the powerful words of St. John Paul II, "The human being is always unique and unrepeatable, somebody thought of and chosen from eternity, some called and identified by his own name."[26] This incredible truth has the power to transform our lives—if we truly believe it and affirm it in our daily activities, in how we speak to ourselves, how we pray, and how we dress.

When we take time to explore our personal style, we can begin learning who we are on a deeper level. Clothing can help us to see ourselves and who we have been called to be more clearly—a person of infinite value. Clothing that dignifies us and expresses the unique beauty of our souls can transform our perception of who we are and who we are called to be. The most important benefit is the transformation of our relationship with God. Not only do we begin to recognize the truth of being made in his image, but we finally understand that since God made us in his image, he must really, deeply love each of us. In his infinite power and goodness, he wanted each of us to exist—so we have infinite value. This truth has the power to reconstruct any false ideas we have of our identity. The more you invest in recognizing and expressing the unrepeatable, unique beauty of your soul and learn to honor your God-given body, the more you grow in understanding of your inherent worth.

Personal style is not commonly associated with growing in faith, but understood through a theological lens, it is a tool for building our relationship with God. Personal style is usually seen as superficial and inwardly facing, but when used to dignify your body and to reveal the unseen beauty of your soul, it has a big-picture impact, one that leads the individual to contemplate his or her identity through the eyes of God. The more we know that we have been made in the image of God, the more we know who God is. Most significantly, the more we recognize the love of the Father who has willed us into existence, the more we are able to return that love to him. The more you see yourself as God sees you, the more your life is changed.

Ultimately, personal style is not about the clothes. It is not about having the best outfit; it is not about looking cute all the time or being fashionable. It is about using the way we physically express ourselves as a tool to know ourselves so that we may come to know God. Our identity is not found in how we look but in how we were made. But we are called to dress in a way that helps us to learn *how* God made us, so we can grow in our relationship with him.

THE BODY, MADE IN THE IMAGE

We know that the clothes we wear have an impact on our psychology (and vice versa), but is there a connection between the things we wear and our spiritual self? This is where the transcendent nature of art meets the transcendent nature of the body. One remark from *Letter to Artists* echoes an important quote from the Theology of the Body, connecting the significance of art with the human body, which is crucial for our study of style. As St. John Paul II says, a key element of art is the act of making visible the invisible: "Art must make perceptible, and as far as possible attractive, the world of the spirit, of the invisible, of God."[27] If you recall in the first part of this book where I had my "aha!" moment in my Theology of the Body class, the quote that stuck out was, "The body, and only the body, makes visible the invisible. The spiritual and the divine."[28]

OK, so let's look at these two quotes side by side:

"Art must make perceptible, and as far as possible attractive, the world of the spirit, of the invisible, of God."

"The body, and only the body, makes visible the invisible. The spiritual and the divine."

Let's break them down a little more:

1. Art makes the invisible perceptible—so art makes visible the divine.

2. The body makes visible the invisible—so the body makes visible the divine.

The key takeaway here is the theme of "making visible the invisible." In these two quotes, St. John Paul II says that art and the body make visible the divine. Ultimately, art and the human body both reveal God. This makes a strong argument for the theological significance of the clothing we place on our bodies. If our clothing can be true, creative expressions of art, then the combination of the human body with clothing makes personal style an incredible opportunity to share the beauty of the human person, made in God's image.

The human body is the culmination of artistic creation. How? Well, because of the Incarnation. The Second Person of the Trinity chose to take on a human nature, body and soul, in Jesus. God chose the body of our Blessed Mother to be Jesus' tabernacle. This is the ultimate example of the beauty of God's creation—and it took place in the human body. As St. John Paul II writes, "In becoming man, the Son of God has introduced into human history all the evangelical wealth of the true and the good, and with this he has also unveiled a new dimension of beauty."[29] At times, we can subconsciously see the human body as a detraction from the spiritual, as something that is "bad" or opposed to our souls. But our bodies are truly imbued with beauty, truth, and goodness because we are children of the Father and brothers and sisters of Jesus, who became one of us.

As we have seen, true art reveals God. But how exactly does the human body reveal God? Sometimes in Catholic circles, we use the phrase "made in the image of God" without fully understanding how. We accept this truth without really understanding it. How are we made in the image of God? Luckily, the Theology of the Body presents us with an anthropology of the human person, and St. John Paul II explains the origins of our being in relation to God.

First, John Paul II discusses the creation of man and the nature of the body. In Genesis 1:26, we read, "Then God said, 'Let us make man in our image, after our likeness.'" This leads to Genesis 2:7, "Then the LORD God formed man of dust from the ground, and breathed into his nostrils the breath of life; and man became a living soul." Essentially, being made in God's "image and likeness" means that we have been endowed with intellect and free will. Our bodies, though, manifest God's image to the world. Now, it is not obvious that our bodies reveal God. After all, God is a divine, spiritual (i.e., non-corporeal) being who exists outside of space and time, while we are corporal beings who exist within—and are limited by—space and time. So how can we say our bodies, the very thing that makes us different from God, express his image in us?

As St. John Paul II explains, "Man is a subject not only by his self-consciousness and self-determination, but also based on his own body. The structure of this body is such that it permits him to be the author of genuinely human activity. In this activity, the body expresses the person."[30] The whole human person is expressed through the body. Everything that God distinctly decided for man to be, created in his image and likeness, is quite literally *in* the body.

We see this in Genesis, when Adam names the animals and finds no being like himself: "Man, formed in this way, belongs to the visible world, he is a body among bodies ... The body, by which man shares in the visible created world, makes him at the same time aware of being 'alone.' His body made this evident to him."[31] In his recognition of being different from the animals, he discovers that he possesses self-consciousness and that he is alone in his kind.

In the Theology of the Body, St. John Paul II refers to humanity's "original solitude," stating, "One can affirm with certainty that man thus formed has at the same time the awareness and consciousness of the meaning of his own body."[32] This act of identification and recognition of being "alone" reveals his consciousness, i.e., his soul. This is the first explanation of the relationship between the body and soul in the Bible. As John Paul clarifies, "Consciousness of the body seems to be identical in this case with the discovery of the complexity of One's Own structure, which in the end, based on a philosophical anthropology, consists in the relation between soul and body."[33] By being conscious of his body and his "aloneness," Adam also discovers the complexity of his being; essentially, he discovers his soul. We see here that the body and soul are inseparable in the creation of man.

But man's discovery of self doesn't end there! In Genesis 2:18, God says, "It is not good for the man to be alone. I will make a suitable partner for him"—Eve. When Adam discovers Eve and declares, "Flesh from my flesh and bone from my bones," he realizes that he is not alone, which helps him to further recognize his identity as someone made in the Image. In discovering the humanity of Eve, he discovers his own. St. John Paul II explains, "The expression 'Flesh of my flesh' takes on precisely this meaning: the body reveals man."[34] Adam discovers Eve's humanity through her body, helping him to further understand his own. As St. John Paul II says, "Thus, the created man finds himself from the first moment of his existence before God in search of his own being, as it were; one could say, in search of his own definition; today one would also say, in search of his own 'identity.'"[35] Upon his creation, man is immediately searching for the meaning of his identity—body and soul—yearning for his Maker.

Even in today's secular culture, we see examples of this. "Finding yourself" has become a cliche we laugh at whenever a twenty-something sets out to define his or her identity after college. But at the core of a person's search for purpose is a confused soul who is seeking the Creator, just as Adam was. Adam wasn't left in confusion though. God created Eve, whose existence allowed Adam to discover the meaning of both their identities before God.

St. John Paul II clarifies, "In this first expression of the man, 'flesh from my flesh' contains also a reference to that by which that body is authentically human and thus to that which determines man as a person, that is, as a being that is, also in its bodiliness, similar to God."[36] That means that through Adam and Eve's bodily recognition and discovery of their humanity, they were led to an even greater discovery. Through recognizing their nature, they realize that they are similar to God and therefore made in his image. It is thanks to the body–soul unity that man is able to arrive at this conclusion. Without the body, he could not have been able to notice his difference from the animals and without his soul he would not be able to discover anything beyond the material. As the body reveals man's distinct nature as a composite being—that is, an inseparable unity of body and soul—it also reveals God, the ultimate source of man's nature. St. John Paul II explains that it is also through man's body that the image of God is revealed: "In Man, created in the image of God, the very sacramentality of creation, the sacramentality of the world, was thus in some way revealed."[37]

How incredible is that? God reveals himself through his creation of man. So we see how we are created in his image through our body–soul unity thanks to Adam's differentiation between himself and the animals. But how deep does "being made in

God's image" go? As we will see, it encompasses every aspect of who we are.

MASCULINITY AND FEMININITY

Many in our culture today hold that masculinity and femininity are merely social constructs. Well, it turns out the masculinity and femininity of our bodies have significance for how we communicate to the world the image of God. As St. John Paul II clarifies, "Man, whom God created 'male' and 'female,' bears the divine image impressed in the body 'from the beginning'; man and woman constitute, so to speak, two diverse ways of 'being a body' that are proper to human nature in the unity of this image."[38] But what does it mean to be "two diverse ways of being a body"? And what do they have to do with the unity of God's image?

First, we need to understand why man was made male and female, as this helps us to see why masculinity and femininity are so incredibly important for how we live God's image completely. It was necessary for both Adam and Eve to exist so they may *both* reflect the image of God. God contains all perfections of unity of masculinity and femininity within himself—though, as a pure Spirit, he is neither male nor female. We were made masculine and feminine so that we may come together, in union with each other, to reflect the communion that exists in the Trinity.

Being made male and female is part of God's plan to make mankind in his image. We are different, equal, and, most importantly, complementary. John Paul II said, "As two complementary dimensions of self-knowledge and self-determination and, at the same time, two complementary ways of being conscious of the meaning of the body."[39] When united, man and woman become one. This makes man and woman the perfect match in every sense. This is what St. John Paul II means when he says that "man and woman constitute two diverse ways of 'being a body' that are proper to human nature in the unity of this image."

This speaks multitudes about the profound relationship between man and woman. We are not meant to exist alone, and one sex isn't better than the other—but truly, man and woman are fully actualized in one another. There is an evangelizing element to this relationship, where man gains a better understanding of his masculinity through woman's femininity and vice versa. How? Just look back at Genesis where man was immediately in search of his identity after realizing he was alone. Adam discovered his identity in discovering Eve's. Discovering their identity in one another led them to discover their identity in God. The relationship between man and woman is meant to bring each other to the Creator.

Consider relationships between the men and women you know. Think of a couple who brings out the best in each other, a couple that has grown together through love, hard work, and sacrifice for the other. There is something important to be said about the special complementarity between man and woman, the way in which they are drawn together by the essence of their being. A kismet force that seems to surpass mere biology and makes you say, "Wow, they really were *made* for each other." Well, they were!

Have you ever witnessed a man become completely dazzled by the presence of a certain woman? Consider the face of a groom watching his bride walk down the aisle. This encounter is not unlike Adam meeting Eve for the first time. He finds himself before this woman, moved to his core simply because of who she is. It changes everything he knows about himself and his relationship with God. When men and women encounter each other, they are constantly reliving this experience to different degrees. The relationship between man and woman is for their betterment, to help each other discover the truth of their identity and to aid in each other's journey for heaven.

Men and women make sense biologically. They physically "fit together" and have the ability to produce offspring. But it also makes sense spiritually. It is a complementarity that reaches through the physical and into the heart of man and woman. As St. John Paul II says, "Man became the image of God not only through his own humanity, but also through the communion of persons, which man and woman formed from the very beginning."[40]

MADE TO FIND OURSELVES IN THE GIFT OF SELF

So mankind was made for communion, but why did he have to be made that way? Being made in God's image means that we also reflect his giving nature. After all, God wanted to bring mankind into existence so that we may share eternity with him. He made us purely out of love, a love that stems from the endless selfless gift that is constantly being exchanged between the Father, Son, and Holy Spirit. We did not need to exist, but he freely created us out of love (CCC 1) as an outpouring of, and ultimately a sharing in, the divine love present within the Trinity. God created our body–soul unity so we may live out that selfless love with each other. On a physical and spiritual level, we do this through the spousal union where man and woman make a vow and give themselves to one another in sincere gift of self. This act of selfless gift reflects the Trinity, allowing us to partake in "the economy of Truth and Love."

In John 17:21-22, Jesus prayed to the Father concerning man, "that all may be one ... as we are one." True to his nature, God freely gave man an opportunity to partake in this eternal love. As stated before, God exists in a never-ending communion of love shared between the Father, Son, and Holy Spirit. He *is* love. By simply being made in the image of this wondrous God, we too participate in his unitive love—we are called to self-gift so we can partake in the ultimate goodness found in living in communion with others and God himself. Our call to unity is an inherited trait. This makes folksy phrases such as "Like father, like son," "The apple doesn't fall far from the tree," and "A chip off the ole' block" take on new meaning. As St. John Paul II says, "The function of the image is that of mirroring the one who is the model, of reproducing its own prototype."[41] Our bodies are imprinted with this identity from the beginning. The gift is present within us from the moment we are conceived because it is the essence and core of our being.

But how necessary is the fulfillment of this innate orientation toward unity? In his Theology of the Body, John Paul II quotes Vatican II's document *Gaudium et Spes* to illustrate the importance of living in communion: "This likeness reveals that man, who is the only creature on earth which God willed for itself, cannot fully find himself except through a sincere gift of himself."[42]

The key takeaway is this truth of "self-gift." We only discover ourselves through a sincere gift of self. Since we have been made in the image of God—who is the actual source and meaning of "gift"—in order to truly discover ourselves, we have to *give* ourselves. This makes sense when we consider the person and life of Jesus Christ, who became the ultimate gift through his sacrifice on the cross, so the gates of heaven may be open to us. He loved us so much that he became one of us, so that we would be able to partake in eternity with him and the communion of persons. This is the ultimate self-gift. "You shall love your neighbor as yourself ... Love therefore is the fulfillment of the law" (Romans 13:9–10; see also 1 John 4:20). To understand real love (and is there any other purpose in life?), we must understand sacrifice—that is, self-gift.

Most of us know that with great love comes great sacrifice. Any parent could tell you this. In an act of great love, parents give to their children even when this means dying to themselves. Most parents will also tell you this selfless love is also one of the most fulfilling experiences and that it changed them for the better. Evidence of this participation in the economy of love is the ability for man and woman to create new life through their union. Again, this reflects the selflessly loving and creative nature of God himself who chose to bring mankind into creation as his children. A husband and wife's love creates new life, in cooperation with God. This is the most obvious physical example of how mankind lives out their nature for unity through their bodies.

However, we live this out every day, whether we are married or not. While marriage is the divinely intended way masculinity and femininity is lived out sexually, single people are called to live out their masculinity and femininity as well. God said, "Love thy neighbor," and this goes for every single person too. We have been discussing how we have been made in God's image and likeness, but this is not limited to those who are married. It is present within each of us from the beginning because each of us has intellect and will, so our bodies express the image of God.

At this point you may be wondering, "How in the world does any of this relate to personal style?" Trust me, it all connects, so hang in there!

Many of us go through life having no clue about our perennial call to unity or how this is reflected in our actions in our everyday lives. (Do you see where I am going with this?) As St. John Paul writes, "In the evolution of ordinary human existence, [even if] little attention is paid to these essential experiences ... they are so intermingled with the ordinary things of life that we do not generally notice their extraordinary character."[43] There is so much depth of our nature that "man does not perceive it in his own everyday life." Wow. This should make us look at our daily activities a little differently, no? Are you now wondering what things you do every day that reflect your call to union?

Think about genuinely friendly conversations with strangers on the train platform, sharing a cat video you know your mom would love, cooking a meal for your boyfriend or husband, listening to a friend who is stressed about work, giving your sister a back massage, offering your last Oreo to your roommate, or reading a story to your niece. All of us have been imbued with an innate desire to give ourselves to others so we can be in union with them. From being a child looking to make his or her first friend, to a young adult seeking a spouse, to a grandparent wanting multitudes of grandchildren, we are a communion-based people.

Sometimes our call to unity is more noticeable when we feel the lack of communion in our lives. Consider days spent alone, where you craved the company of another. Think of times you missed a certain friend or desired to find a core group of friends in your town. Or perhaps when you longed to meet a special someone while scrolling through a dating app. This call to communion is written not only within the structure of our bodies but also in our souls. It comes from a deep place within us and pours out of us in everything we do. In every phase of life, we live out God's words in Genesis, "It is not good that the man should be alone" (Genesis 2:18).

We want connection, companionship, and family. At the crux of it, we want to find ourselves in reciprocal self-gift. We want to love and be loved in an authentic way. This desire does not just come from a superficial need for happy-fuzzy feelings of love or attention. Rather, the source comes from the deep pull to partake in something greater than oneself. Our desire to be in union with others comes from the innate desire to be in union with God himself. This desire for union with God is revealed in everything we do, whether we realize it or not. Many of us may feel the obvious call to unity with others through romantic relationships, as well as the desire for a family of our own. But we make visible our invisible call to unity in every aspect of life, not just through romantic relationships and the spousal union.

This brings us back to art. As we read in St. John Paul II's *Letter to Artists*, artists disclose their personality, history, and identity as a child of God through swipes of paint, etches of charcoal, or the melody of a song. This physical expression reflects that innate orientation to self-gift just as our daily encounters with others do. Let's recall the artists who share a part of who they are through their work. As St. John Paul II writes, "Through his works, the artist speaks to others and communicates with them. The history of art, therefore, is not only a story of works produced but also a story of men and women. Works of art speak of their authors; they enable us to know their inner life."[44] This act of artistic expression is part of self-gift.

SELF-GIFT THROUGH EXPRESSION OF THE SOUL THROUGH STYLE

Now let's consider a daily activity that involves both an encounter with others *and* the expression of self. It begins the moment you get out of bed, open your closet, and choose an outfit for the day. Yes, the way we dress is another way we reveal our perennial call to self-gift.

As we have seen, personal style is a unique expression of the self on both a personal and psychological level. Now let's reframe that through the concept of self-gift. When we dress in a way that makes visible the invisible beauty of our souls, dignifies our bodies, and communicates the Creator who created us, we are communicating the wholeness of who we are with others. We are offering a visible representation of our identity as children of God. The powerful thing about personal style is that it is an opportunity to simultaneously communicate our individuality, while also pointing back toward our origin: God. This is a gift to those around us because it allows them to encounter who we are in an authentic way that reveals our identity in God. As we defined earlier, personal style is an opportunity to make visible the invisible. Personal style combines St. John Paul II's messages in the Theology of the Body and his *Letter to Artists*: the body and the clothes we place on it can be an authentic artistic expression of the human person made in God's image. In other words, it makes visible the invisible.

This can all come across as very cerebral, but let's bring it back to earth. What does this all look like in our day-to-day lives? Consider a time a friend or family member of yours got dressed up, where the time and effort she put into her ensemble and the care to reflect the best version of herself was evident. Maybe it was Christmas when your sister emerged at the top of the stairs, and you were taken aback by how beautiful she was in her midnight Mass dress. Or perhaps a time you met up with a date who clearly took the time to dress his best for you, and it made him glow in a special way. You might even recall a time you were struck by the apparel of a complete stranger, which communicated who they were even though you didn't know them. It is not just the clothes that are making an impact, but the person that radiates through them.

Now, think of a time when you took the time to choose items that communicated your authentic self, when getting dressed wasn't simply practical, but a process of selecting items to create an outfit that made your chest swell, put a pep in your step, and made you walk taller. An outfit that made you feel like the best version of yourself, a time where your outfit influenced your whole day. How did it affect you? Maybe you walked down the street, more inclined to smile at people passing by, engaging in a lighthearted conversation with your cafe barista. Maybe you took a quick snapshot of your outfit for Instagram. These were important moments that helped you to recognize the truth of your identity, encouraging you to live it out in your daily life.

Being filled with confidence and self-assurance in our identity spills out into our encounters with others. We are naturally more inclined to share who we are when we feel confident in who we are. It is impactful when we give ourselves to others in these seemingly small encounters of community. The things we wear can empower us to share more readily who we are with others through that confidence, but it also has an unspoken power of communicating who we are through prints, colors, textures, and silhouettes—without us even saying a word.

The goal is to develop a personal style that makes tangible the intangible beauty of your soul, a visual representation of the unrepeatable way you were made. What a gift it is to share this with others! A unique invitation to those who encounter us— that they may come to know the unseen parts of who we are through a tangible expression of self. In this way, personal style is a connector of people, a force for unity and communion. We do not dress only for ourselves but for those around us, so that they may come to know us in a real way and have insight into our true identity; that they may meet the parts of who we are that we cannot express in words; they may see the beauty of our souls manifested in the beauty of our ensembles.

St. John Paul II said that art enables viewers to encounter the personality of the artists. As mentioned, it seems fair to consider personal style as an artistic endeavor, a famous medium of expressing one's personality. "Expressing yourself" through style has often been written off as a marketing tool popular brands use on identity-seeking teenagers, but it may be more theologically significant than you think. Why? Personality is evidence for the human soul. Any expression of personality, including through the way we dress, should therefore be taken seriously.

So how is the personality evidence for the soul? Reason defines man as separate from the irrational animals, and the presence of the soul is made known. The inner workings of who he is is evident. Through this interior processing, he recognizes that the animals cannot think and process reality as he does. In a word, man possesses a self-reflective consciousness. This interior self is something each of us is familiar with. It is how we experience ourselves. It is how you are absorbing these very words, remembering past experiences, developing opinions, and thinking of how any of this applies to your life. The intimate complexity of our internal self is the ultimate testament to our individuality. A one-of-a-kind being, never to be repeated. Utterly distinct because you are *you*, and no one else.

Personality is an exterior expression of the individuality of the human soul. Are your friends exactly alike in their personalities? No. Because the diversity of their personalities points toward the source—which is their individual, unique, and unrepeatable soul. "The body makes visible the invisible, the spiritual and the divine." How incredible it is to be given the gift of physical expression? To share our intangible souls through our tangible bodies—to jump for joy, to dance in celebration, to offer a sympathetic expression to someone who needs it, to share our personality through our bodies? What we choose to wear can aid in this expression. Small style choices that seem insignificant actually reveal those unseen parts of who you are.

What does this look like, you ask? Let me give an example that involves myself, a used clothing fair in a warehouse in Brooklyn, and a Hawaiian shirt. Yes, you read that right, I said "Hawaiian shirt." So, I was wandering through this warehouse when I came across a billowing, blue Hawaiian shirt with silver white lilies on it. It nearly screamed, "Hey! We're made for each other!" from the hanger. From the bright powdery blue hue to its funky floral print and mandarin collar, it was the ultimate "me" item.

But what does that mean? What is "me"? How can we describe the self without pointing toward that intangible soul which animates our bodies? It is what defines us as distinct individuals at the moment of conception. It is your essence, your "you-ness." Discovering clothes that reflect this unrepeatable "you-ness" is special and unique to every person. It is an attraction to beauty while simultaneously expressing the beauty of your soul. It is finding a match—clothes that match your body and soul. Clothes that help you to recognize your soul and the dignity of your body, helping you to see just how unrepeatable and important you are in the eyes of God. And there it is ... personal style is evidence for the human soul.

This reality makes a huge impact simply on how we see ourselves. The more we choose clothes that remind us of our unique and unrepeatable souls, the more we understand the worth of our being. As we come to understand our worth, the more our lives are impacted, changing how we behave and engage with others. As St. John Paul II, quoting Nicholas of Cusa, writes, "Creative art, which it is the soul's good fortune to entertain, is not to be identified with that essential art which is God himself, but is only a communication of it and a share in it."[45] Mankind is God's greatest work of art, and when the artist creates, he communicates and shares in God's art. When we dress in a way that celebrates the soul and dignifies the body, we share God's art—his creation. The more man is exposed to the beauty of art, revealing the crucial elements of the human person, the more it functions as an evangelizing power, helping others to recognize the existence of their own souls and their relationship with their Creator.

Consider the concept behind trends. Although the idea behind something that is "trendy" has been monopolized and trivialized by big-box brands looking to cash in by creating "of-the-moment" looks, we are able to see how a person's personal style can influence another. The other day I was mesmerized by the beauty of a woman's ensemble in a shop. She was wearing a pair of sleek flares, square-toe crocodile boots underneath, a cream knit turtleneck, and a cream leather coat with fur around the sleeves and collar. I was drawn in by how she was expressing the beauty of her individuality through these items. In her own self-expression, I saw elements of myself as well. This is the power of style. While I didn't want to copy her style item by item, the beauty of her clothing choices made me remember my own unique style. She made me remember that I too am a beautiful, one-of-a-kind woman created by the Creator and I desired to express that back to my God and my community.

St. John Paul II describes the spiritual benefits of man's artistic pursuits, "For him, art offers both a new dimension and an exceptional mode of expression for his spiritual growth. Through his works, the artist speaks to others and communicates with them."[46] Art is not necessary for God's self-actualization and growth, but art *is* necessary for man's. Art is a method by which man is able to express who God is to the other. For in expressing the depths of his own being, made in God's image, he also expresses who God is. In turn, anyone who encounters this art is pushed to realize that they too are made in the image of God, which strengthens our understanding of our relationship with the Creator.

THE SPECIAL GIFT OF FEMININE BEAUTY AND THE DIVINE

Beauty that leads to the divine isn't something only great pieces of artwork can possess but also human beings—specifically, women. In fact, beauty is a gift that has been uniquely bestowed upon women. This is evident in our everyday lives.

Consider the culture in which we live. Even within the world of portrait art, the primary subject is typically women. Male artists have had female muses for centuries; consider the *Mona Lisa*, *The Girl with the Pearl Earring*, and *The Birth of Venus*, to name a few.

Entire industries revolve around the beauty of women. Fashion magazines have "cover girls" and "supermodels," and clothing brands cater toward women with entire fashion weeks and designer labels dedicated to emphasizing the beauty of the feminine form. Not to mention the makeup industry which existed solely for women for decades. Why is this? Why are women at the center of all things dealing with physical beauty? Why not men?

To put it plainly, women *are* more beautiful than men. Women are the fairer sex. Women tend to have softer bodies, curves, and an inviting openness to our facial features that emphasizes our eyes, lips, and cheeks—features that captivate and more expressively communicate their internal feminine identity. If you are a man reading this, you might reply, "Hey! What about us?!" And yes, of course, men are beautiful in their own way. But their physical stature, sharpness, strength, angularity, and coarseness do not express the same softness and openness as the woman that speaks to her unique internal nature. It makes sense for women to be the fairer sex because of the very nature of her being.

Influential Catholic philosopher Alice von Hildebrand touched on this, "God has indeed created women to be beautiful. Their charm, lovableness, and beauty exercise a powerful attraction on the male sex, and it should be so. It is noteworthy that feminine loveliness contradicts the biological norm, usually that the male animal is more beautiful than the female one. No one would deny that women are or can be beautiful. It is not by accident that they are called "the fairer sex.'"[47]

As von Hildebrand states, it is no accident that women are the more beautiful sex. But why? Why do women defy the biological norm? Why have women been chosen to be beautiful?

If we consider our earlier reflections on the purpose of art and the beauty that draws mankind to contemplate the divine, femininity is the ultimate example of earthly beauty that leads to the divine. In fact, beauty is a special gift specifically bestowed upon womankind because it draws all of mankind to contemplate and even encounter the divine. Femininity and beauty go hand-in-hand.

The beauty of a church is not unlike the beauty of a woman. Gilded cathedrals—with ornate ceilings, towering stained glass windows, and intricately designed tabernacles—function as a manifestation of divine beauty. The tangible beauty of the church draws its children to contemplate the beauty of the divine. Similarly, the physical beauty of the woman is a manifestation of her greatly dignified role in creation. The beauty of a woman is even greater than the beauty of great works of art, cathedrals, and glorious landscapes because she even more profoundly makes visible the beauty of the human person who is made in the image of God.

Let's reflect on the Blessed Mother, who is the woman of all women and became the tabernacle of the living God. Our Lady was the first church, the first glorious cathedral, and the first tabernacle to house God himself. It is Our Lady who brings souls to her Son every day. It is she whom we look upon as the ultimate feminine who draws humanity to the divine.

The physical beauty of woman reflects her role as co-creator of life with God. A woman's beauty reflects the closeness of her role with the Creator and the divine. In a sense, as von Hildebrand points out, a woman's beauty contradicts the biological norm. Why? Because from the beginning, God chose women to be the vessel through which he creates life. The woman's body has an even greater dignity and closeness to divinity because her womb is touched by God himself every time she conceives new life. Her beauty is a sign of her privileged role. Beauty is imbued in her biology because her being is so intimately connected with the divine.

Her physical beauty is a consequence of her highly esteemed nature, and it does serve a greater purpose. But her beauty isn't merely physical. In choosing women as a co-creator, the woman's entire nature, and being has been raised. Von Hildebrand's *The Privilege of Being a Woman* explores the special role of women as she speaks about "the beauty of femininity as coming out of God's loving hand, and the glorious mission assigned to it when fecundated by the supernatural."[48]

This unique mission permeates a woman's identity and is most evident in the beauty of her heart. Von Hildebrand uses St. Scholastica and her brother, St. Benedict, as an example. She recounts St. Benedict described his sister as "having the stronger love, she had the stronger power."[49] Von Hildebrand also argues that women, more than men, grasp intuitively the meaning and value of suffering.[50] This is unsurprising as women tend to be more empathetic and compassionate, a side effect of their profound capacity to love. This is an inherited trait, a byproduct of being co-creator with God himself.

This immense capacity to love is something God shared with women, solidifying the uniquely collaborative nature that she shares with him. Not just collaborative in the way that she physically creates life with God, but collaborative in that she is given a heart that can love unconditionally, as God loves. Of course, men do have the capacity to suffer and love unconditionally; they are called to model their lives on the love that Christ has for the Church. But a woman, by virtue of her femininity, is uniquely equipped to bear suffering in her being.

Von Hildebrand also pointed out that women are more inclined to see the significance of the whole person rather than abstractly viewing a person for their parts. This means that women are naturally able to grasp the whole value of the human person more easily than men, allowing them to love more readily. Women have a natural ability to prioritize things of true value, respecting the hierarchy of living things above all else. As von Hildebrand stated, "Christ is the life of the soul, and women, who have the sublime mission of giving life, intuitively weave this principle into their daily lives."[51]

This might all sound very metaphysical, but let's consider examples in our personal lives. Think of a time you were homesick. Maybe you were away at a sleepover, at camp, or even in college. Most of the time, we aren't homesick—but "momsick." We miss our mothers, not a physical space. Truly, home is where your mom is. Or consider a time a family member, a friend, child, or even a stranger, was in need and your heart instinctively reacted to try and help—that gut-wrenching pull to heal, soothe, comfort, to give emotional shelter to those who need it. Those who find themselves underneath the umbrella of a woman's love are guided by her love to encounter the source of love in God himself. Like the Church, she shelters and guides her children to the love of her Bridegroom.

A woman's body is a home. She is physically a home to the children she bears, but even more importantly, her heart is a home for those she loves. In marriage, a woman opens her heart and body to God, her spouse, and her children. She opens her heart to her loved ones, and they find rest in her love. Her love is a special extension of the Creator's love. A mother's heart is a sacred place because it is a piece of God's heart—the only place we can find true rest. The woman is given a heart that is an extension of Christ's heart. In knowing the love of a woman, all of mankind is blessed with an earthly bridge and example of Christ's pure, endless love. Love is a woman's true beauty; it reflects God, who is Love.

What an incredible gift this is, or as von Hildebrand said, a privilege, to be chosen as God's ally in bringing mankind to the divine. As John Paul II has said, "These words are a eulogy of motherhood, of femininity, of the feminine body in its typical expression of creative love."[52]

When we reflect on femininity through this lens, it makes all the sense in the world why women tend to be very creative. Women are inherently creative because it is in our very nature, our very bodies, to physically create. This is manifested on an everyday level where women are attuned to the physical expression of beauty. Consider even seemingly silly things, like Pinterest and the excitement most women feel when mood-boarding and collecting inspiration for their home, wardrobe, and lifestyle.

Many women can attest to the thrill of exploring a thrift or antique shop in search of hidden gems that will later help make their house a home. Women are also much more likely to find joy in discovering their personal style and expressing their unique identity through their clothes. It makes sense that the fashion and beauty industry is catered toward women, since women are naturally attuned to authentic creativity and self-donation through their efforts to communicate the beauty of God via artistic expression.

With this gift comes great opportunity and responsibility. Von Hildebrand makes the distinction between "authentic creativity" and the superficial pursuit of shallow "self-expression." Our goal when dressing should be authentic creativity, not an attempt to reduce oneself to an object (but more on that later.) The goal should always be to express the fullness of our being, rather than succumbing to the pitfalls of worldliness and superficial promises of fulfillment that reduce human happiness to merely physical appeal. Von Hildebrand explains that because of woman's highly privileged role, she's more in danger of misusing her gifts—specifically, misusing the evangelizing power of her beauty for "own destruction and that of others."[53]

FEMININE BEAUTY UNDER ATTACK

Hand-in-hand with this gift comes a unique mission. Von Hildebrand even said, "Woman is one of the grand instruments of which Providence makes use to prepare the way for civilization."[54] A woman's exterior and interior beauty is a tool for bringing mankind to the divine. Of course, with anything that is true, beautiful, and good, the Devil makes it his mission to attack it. Woman has been the Devil's nemesis since the beginning of time. Von Hildebrand touches on this: "It is luminous that Eve is the enemy *par excellence* because being the mother of the living, she is Satan's arch enemy for he was 'a murderer from the beginning' and hates life."[55] When we look around at our culture, we see evidence of this attack in the pains of our generation(s) in areas that have to do with new life. Broken families, abortion, gender identity confusion, and perverse sexuality all trace back to the initial corruption of femininity.

The pervasive attack on women is most obvious in our media. Entire industries revolve around the corruption of femininity and the exploitation of beauty. This is most clear in pornography, but we encounter it whenever we see women and young girls in the media posing in suggestive positions in small pieces of fabric. Our digital age has certainly made it easier to reduce a woman's role to appealing to sexual appetites, but the attempt to separate a woman's body from her soul has been present since the Fall. In fact, we can go back to Genesis to get at the source of today's problem.

We all know the story: man, woman, serpent, apple, and the Fall. But why was the Fall so catastrophic? Why was eating the fruit such a big deal? Why did it affect our relationships with one another and the way we see our bodies? What the heck happened to mankind in the Fall?!

Let's set up the original context of God and man's relationship so we can better understand what was lost.

We exist purely out of God holding us in existence because he loves us. When Adam and Eve doubted God's love, the ultimate gift, and chose to reject God's love by believing the Devil's lies, it affected the very core of man's ability to relate with each other and to relate with God. It impacted the way men and women love each other. Mankind is relational, so the fracturing of man's relationship with God had lasting effects on our relationships with others also.

As St. John Paul II explains, "By casting doubt in his heart on the deepest meaning of the gift, that is, on love as the specific motive of creation and of the original covenant, man turns his back on God-Love, on the 'Father.' He in some sense casts him from his heart."[56] Man detaches his heart and cuts it off from that which "comes from the Father." This is the ability to have true, effortless union that extends from their union with God.

But what does that mean for us?

Think of unity as beginning in God and flowing down to Adam and Eve and then flowing back to God again. It was an effortless, organic relationship that existed in the constant reception and return of the gift of self. But when man doubted God's gift, it disrupted the entire flow of the exchange between God, Adam, and Eve. When Adam and Eve broke the covenant by doubting God's love for them and acting out of selfishness, they lost the ability to have the same unity with each other.

Think about it: When there is distrust of someone's selfless love and then the solidification of that distrust with betrayal, the relationship is no longer reciprocal—and the gift of love is no longer freely given because it can no longer be freely received. As man and woman turned away from God, they turned toward the world, and in so doing, they allowed concupiscence to damage their nature.

What is "concupiscence" exactly? Concupiscence is the complete opposite of selfless gift. It is the inclination to sin. Concupiscence is the state in which man and woman find themselves after rejecting the gift and committing original sin. It attacks the very thing that raised man and woman above the animals: their ability to recognize each other's true identity as someone made in the image of God. Remember when Adam discovered his identity in the creation of Eve and vice versa? This original revelation and understanding of their true identity before God transformed after their rejection of the gift.

In their original innocence, man and woman selflessly gave themselves to one another—reaffirming their identity as children of God. Concupiscence distorts the viewer's perception to see another as an object for themselves, instead as a subject, as a person. "Then the eyes of both were opened, and they knew that they were naked; and they sewed fig leaves together and made themselves aprons" (Genesis 3:7).

Suddenly, man and woman can no longer grasp the fullness of the other's being. Prior to the Fall, they intuitively understood themselves and one another as a body–soul unity. After the Fall, the eyes of their hearts were obscured, and they struggled to see beyond the body and grasp the totality of each other's being.

Their sexuality, the very thing that allowed them to know the fullness of the other's being, became a hurdle. Cut off from the supernatural gift, man and woman are alienated from the fullness of the good that was intended for them. The original power of communicating themselves to each other has been shattered, and they are estranged from each other in self-destructive shame.

Although a product of the Fall, shame sheds light on our study of the Theology of Style and the power of clothing in dignifying the body. St. John Paul II describes shame as having a redemptive element: "Shame has a twofold meaning: it indicates the threat to the value and at the same time it preserves this value in an interior way."[57]

While shame came about through sin, there is a positive that can be gained from it. Shame is a symptom of a deeper wound. Like any symptom, it alerts the sick person to seek out the source of their pain so they can fix it. When we experience hunger pains, this is our body's way of alerting us to eat. When we break a bone, our brain sets off pain alarms to let us know that we are injured. Shame is a symptom of an internal wound that pushes man to find healing. As most of us know, shame feels pretty darn awful. And when we feel that way, we try to figure out why. "Why is this feeling disturbing me so much? Why is it giving me a pit in my stomach? What triggered this reaction in me? How can I get back to *not* feeling this way?"

Shame, like pain, has before and after components. When we are in pain, we remember how it felt *not* to be in pain, and we desire to get back to that original pain-free experience. In remembering ourselves before shame and realizing how awful the state of shame feels, we should naturally seek out ways to regain our pre-shame experience. Shame only exists because we can remember the pre-shame experience. It is not a pointless feeling. Rather, if we feel shame, this is because there is a way to redemption. As St. John Paul II explained, shame preserves the experience of original innocence in man, allowing him to remember what he has lost—to recognize his error and attempt reconstruction. Shame serves as an echo within man's heart, calling him back to restore innocence and his relationship with God.

The existence of shame means that not all is lost.

Despite Adam and Eve's egregious mistake, they were still formed in the image of God, and therefore their hearts would always be called to greater good. Original sin couldn't change the entire nature of their being. They were still made for unity. This *is* the same couple pre-Fall; they are the same community of persons. Their purpose has not changed, but as St. John Paul II explains, they are "threatened by the insatiability of the union and unity, which does not cease to attract man and woman precisely because they are persons, called from eternity to exist 'in communion.'"[58] He goes on to say, "The 'body,' which is constituted in the unity of the personal subject, does not cease to arouse the desires for personal union, precisely due to masculinity and femininity; on the other hand, concupiscence itself simultaneously directs these desires in its own way."

Instead of the body and soul being in seamless harmony and communication with each other, the very nature of the human person began to fight against itself. But while their bodies carry "within [themselves] a constant hotbed of resistance against the spirit," mankind was not entirely cut off from each other. To put it simply, it just got a lot harder. St. John Paul II explains, "The radical change in the original meaning of nakedness lets us presume negative changes in the whole interpersonal relation between man and woman ... What disappears is the simplicity and 'purity' of their original experience, which helped to bring about a singular fullness of mutual self-communication."[59]

Once concupiscence entered the scene, the original ease by which they communicated through their bodies was gone, "What disappeared was the simple and direct self-communion connected with the original experience of reciprocal nakedness." Man and woman's understanding of each other is wrought with miscommunication, struggle, objectification, and pain. But, obviously, the first parents did not just stop communicating with each other through their bodies. They were still called to union with one another, and the human race carried on.

That brings this discussion back to us. What does this mean for men and women in the twenty-first century, many years removed from the original fall of man? Should we just give up and succumb to concupiscence? Is there any hope for reconstructing what we lost? Well, thankfully Jesus Christ came as a man, body and soul, and opened the gates of heaven for us, both body and soul. In sacrificing his own body on the cross, rising from the dead, and offering his body and blood through the Eucharist, Jesus redeems the human body itself. Jesus, in the ultimate self-sacrifice, died for us. He redeemed us, allowing us to be in union with God as originally intended: "That they may all be one; even as you, Father, are in me, and I in you, that they also may be in us" (John 17:21).

SELF-MASTERY AND THE PURSUIT OF HOLINESS

While Baptism cleanses us of original sin, the inclination to sin remains. We feel this on a daily basis, and we encounter it in the world around us. St. John Paul II describes the state of man now: "Man *can* become a gift—that is, man and woman can exist in the relationship of the reciprocal gift of self—if each of them masters himself."[60] Concupiscence still exists and manifests itself as a "constraint of the body," limiting and restricting man's ability for self-mastery. "The beauty that the human body possesses in its male and female appearance, as an expression of the spirit, is obscured."[61]

If you have ever found yourself ogling an attractive person, obsessing over a handsome actor, or crushing on someone you barely know, you may have been struggling to see that person as a whole person. Sometimes this can be innocent and simply point toward the inherited struggle to fully comprehend a person's full identity. But sometimes this obscured view can slip into major mortal sin territory if we don't catch ourselves and fight for self-mastery. A valuable distinction to make here is the difference between desire and lust. It is OK to have a crush or to desire someone. Desire implies the hope of discovering that person emotionally, spiritually, and mentally, whereas lust is the drive to consume and use them. We must employ self-mastery so as to not let healthy desire turn into lust.

This self-mastery can be difficult, especially in a culture that promotes the use of pornography to boys and encourages young girls to "embrace" their sexuality by commodifying their bodies. The secular world tells us that furthering the split between the body and soul is what will satisfy our desire for fulfillment. That human use and selfishness will appease our appetite for God.

It is not hard to find evidence that this way of life is full of emptiness. No amount of casual sex can fulfill the pit of loneliness we feel in our heart of hearts. The following beautiful reality espoused by the fathers of Vatican II may be lost to the modern world, but it is still present within the heart of every human person:

> Indeed, the Lord Jesus, when [he] prayed to the Father, "that all may be one ... as we are one" (John 17:21-22) opened up vistas closed to human reason, for [he] implied a certain likeness between the union of the divine Persons, and the unity of God's children in truth and charity. This likeness reveals that man, who is the only creature on earth which God willed for itself, cannot fully find himself except through a sincere gift of himself.[62]

Even in a fallen state, man and woman will always subconsciously seek the reciprocal communion of persons. Whether we realize it or not, we are constantly striving to satisfy our desire to live out our calling to have true union—even if it can express itself as warped and unhealthy. Nobody does anything purely for the sake of evil; they always perceive a good in what they do, no matter how misguided it may be. Everything we do is an attempt to know ourselves and, ultimately, to know God.

Even though concupiscence continues to obscure our understanding of the value of the whole human person and the body–soul unity, the call is still there. And, truly, our work is cut out for us. St. John Paul II stated, "Man and woman must reconstruct the meaning of the reciprocal ... gift with great effort."[63] Every day we have to work to reconstruct and maintain what we lost. We constantly have to fight against the wound of concupiscence.

Our bodies are not subject to the spirit, they are in resistance with each other because of concupiscence. Knowledge and pursuit of the unity of body and soul is what helps us reconstruct our original innocence. The self-mastery St. John Paul II described is a lesson for how we are called to live our everyday lives. Self-mastery isn't something we suddenly possess, but something we must actively work on in the formation of habits, routine, self-discipline, and personal commitment. Some examples:

- Waking up and going to bed every day at the same time breeds a habit of respecting your bodily need for rest.

- Saying no to another episode and choosing to read instead to feed your mind.

- Closing your laptop or putting down your smartphone when you feel tempted to look at pornography to cultivate sexual respect.

- Committing to speaking without profanity.

- Signing up for that holy hour to invest in your relationship with Christ.

- Praying before bed instead of scrolling through social media.

These are all habits we develop so we can have a healthier relationship with ourselves and others. The goal through any habit is to achieve self-mastery, to unify the body and soul in pursuit of holiness.

The way we dress is one way we can continually fight to remind ourselves of the unity between body and soul, not just in ourselves but also in others. How we express our bodies plays a vital role in self-mastery. On a personal level, how we dress communicates to ourselves that we have a body worthy of respect and a personality worthy of expression. The more we dress to dignify our bodies, the more we internalize that we are indeed individuals of value. The more we communicate to ourselves and others that we are worthy of respect and love, the more it becomes second nature to our perception of ourselves.

MEN AND WOMEN: COMMUNICATION THROUGH CLOTHING

But how we dress is also especially important when it comes to communication between members of the opposite sex.

As we learned, the Fall caused man and woman to lose the initial ease and understanding of each other's identity. Consider how frustrating the differences between men and women are. The saying "men are from Mars, women are from Venus" sometimes seems painfully true.

Why is he so disconnected from his emotions?

Why is she so emotional?

There is a natural difference between men and women that is complementary, yet fraught with frustration and confusion thanks to sin. Yet somehow, men and women are still instinctively drawn to each other, despite our differences. There is a desire to be in union with one another, even when it is hard. Man and woman still want to understand each other. Just as our words and actions are vital for communicating with each other, so is the way we physically express ourselves—including how we dress.

Men and women look different. Now, how is that for a "duh" statement? More notably, though, men and women physically express themselves differently because of their physical and internal differences. All you need to do is walk into a department store to see one side dedicated to bright colors, patterns, billowing fabrics, embellishments, patterns, etc., and the other side dedicated to neutral tones, sturdy fabrics, structured silhouettes, and versatile basics. While trends are currently changing due to gender identity politics and you can see men regularly wearing nail polish now, overall, you can count on a women's section to be the one selling dresses and heels.

The material difference in men and women's clothing points toward an internal truth about masculine and feminine identity. And no, this is not a dated, 1950s perspective of poodle skirts and suspenders. Before you tell me to get back into my time machine, I want to clarify that there is a lot of room for diversity within the respective masculine and feminine genres of clothing. Dressing femininely doesn't look just one stereotypical way, and neither does dressing masculinely.

But overall, men's fashion primarily focuses on structure and silhouette. Consider blazers, button-downs, slacks, jackets, suits, and coats. Men's garments are cut to highlight the angles, lines, broadness, and overall stature of the male body. His clothes are engineered to flatter and emphasize a strong frame. The color palette usually tends toward muted, versatile, neutral tones like tan, olive, navy, white, and black. Men's clothing reflects a masculine nature that is no-fuss, straightforward, and direct. There's an unchanging element to men's style, which contrasts with the ever-moving, flowing, artistic expression of women's style.

Women's clothing has an array of diverse options with dresses, skirts, shorts, capris, culottes, wide-leg pants, flares, tank tops, and blouses, all in different prints, patterns, colors, silhouettes, and embellishments. While women's clothing does focus on flattering the body, it places more value on the expression of the individual woman herself. Womenswear is more likely to draw a woman's attention initially with a fun pleated detail, sleeve ruffle, or floral print. A woman picks up an item that's drawn her with its unique design first, making her wonder, "How does this express who I am as a person? Does this reflect my personality?" Women's fashion is directed at expressing a woman's feminine nature; her essence, her openness, her beauty, her heart, her soul, her *joie de vivre*. It is later, when she puts the garment on in the dressing room, that she considers the garment's structure, asking, "Does this flatter my body?"

In short, women's fashion tends to capture the spirit first—it appeals to the soul, in which women tend to place more value. The expression of women's fashion tends to be more in tune to certain aspects of color, detail, and beauty. Women are more relational and people-centric, and they put more focus on emotions that stem from their interior selves. A woman asks, "How does this dress make me feel? What do my clothes share about my personality with others?" A woman considers how she can best express the beauty of her identity. She finds joy in sharing herself this way. The soul is colorful, vibrant, radiant, complex, and endlessly beautiful. A woman will seek out clothing that manifests this internal reality.

Women's style focuses more on the soul, whereas men's style focuses more on the body. If a man walks (or is dragged) into a store, he may often choose the most simple and straightforward item he can find. A man's expression of self tends to reflect straightforwardness. When he tries it on, he just wants it to fit well and suit his everyday life. An outfit that makes a man feel good about himself tends to involve elements that uphold his body's dignity, emphasizing his physical strength and stature, overall giving him a look of internal nobility and character. Men tend to want to look distinguished, classy, and traditionally masculine. At the heart of masculinity is protective strength, stability, security, consistency, order, and structure. His clothing choices reflect this. This contrasts with the effervescent, creative, bold, and emotionally expressive counterpart of woman.

So here we have two important differences between the physical expression of man and woman—manifestations of the masculine and feminine. These two physical expressions are different, reflecting the internal identity of our respective souls. More importantly, they are wonderfully complementary to each other, just as men and women were made to be. In union with each other, they make a perfect pair, balancing and highlighting each other's strengths. Ideally, they support and bring out the best in each other. In actively dressing to emphasize their inherent masculinity and femininity, men and women can gain a further appreciation for each other's God-given nature.

Because clothing is a non-verbal form of communication that makes visible the invisible identity of a person, the way men and women dress plays a big role in how they are in communion with each other in society.

Regarding self-mastery, as St. John Paul II points out, the way we express ourselves physically can uphold the truth of our being. The way we dress can form a habit of recognizing our own worth, dignity, and unrepeatable identity and allow us to hold others to the standard of treating us as such. It can instruct others on how to view us, treat us, and contemplate our unique identity, made in the image of God. The way we dress should encourage those who encounter us to see us as someone who is willed into existence and has infinite worth. Because as we discussed above, men and women both battle to overcome the hurdle of concupiscence and struggle to see their counterpart as a body–soul unity, and so dressing purposefully is a key tool for the two sexes to understand each other more fully.

Our entire study here in *Theology of Style* is to apply the truths revealed in the Theology of the Body to how we dress and present ourselves every day. In understanding the Theology of the Body, we unlock the very purpose and meaning of our existence—to recognize the capacity in which we were made in God's image as a body–soul unity and how the relationship between man and woman reflects God's own identity in the Trinity. Mankind was created man and woman, and from the beginning they were called to be in union with one another so they may be led to a greater union with God himself. The spousal union of the body and the physical expression of masculinity and femininity tangibly communicate this spiritual reality. This means that the way men and women express themselves, especially physically, is very important. Their physical expression of self points toward an internal, anthropological truth. How man and woman dress can aid in communicating this truth, helping fulfill their call to unity with one another.

As we discussed above, the beauty of a woman has an evangelizing power that allows man to contemplate the divine. Woman can make visible the beauty of femininity to man through the way she physically expresses herself, including how she dresses. Similarly, man can communicate the invisible truths of masculinity through his own sartorial choices. Remember when Adam exclaimed, "bone of my bone, flesh of my flesh"? His encounter with Eve's femininity led him to a greater understanding of his own being and relation to God. In our physical expression of self through clothing, we can reveal to others the depths of our being and give them insight into the profound nature of the human person.

It is interesting to note that Adam and Eve's first garments (aka fig leaves) were worn out of disunion. It initially signified their newfound misunderstanding of the body, a symbol of concupiscence. It is incredible that in the redemption of the body, clothing is now a tool to help men and women grow in understanding of the other's masculine and feminine identity and to fight to reconstruct their original call to unity. The fig leaves signified Adam and Eve hiding from God. By extension, they were hiding from their own identity as made in God's image. They hid through makeshift clothing, covering up their newly damaged human nature. But when we consider the purpose of "style" intellectually, the purpose of dressing is not to conceal, but to reveal, to reveal being made in the image of God. Personal style points toward transcendence, to where God's identity is revealed through man's physical expression.

A brief note: Dressing "masculinely" and dressing "femininely" doesn't mean that women must be relegated to pinks and floral skirts and dresses, or that men must only wear plain, structured suits and basics. I'm not advocating for a society where women and men must look like a Norman Rockwell painting.

Floral prints and the color pink are not inherently feminine, even though it is traditionally seen as such. For example, before the nineteenth century, pink was actually a boy's color, and blue was for girls. Similarly, a man incorporating feminine details into his style does not and cannot change the essence of his being, which is masculine. Similarly, a woman who enjoys wearing men's graphic tees, button-downs, or Levi's, is not suddenly un-feminine. No garment can transform someone's entire being from feminine to masculine. The beauty of personal style is that the individual may take items from fashion history and incorporate them into their own expression of self, further revealing their femininity or masculinity—even if the items are not stereotypically "feminine" or "masculine."

For example, I frequently wear a large second-hand camo jacket. I will often throw it over a long maxi dress or create a peplum shape by belting it at the waist. Instead of this garment making me "manly," it actually highlights my femininity. The contrast of the masculine garment simply emphasizes and complements my feminine identity. It allows for more creative expression that isn't confined to a narrow aesthetic of how a woman "should" dress. Remember, personal style is the opportunity to visually communicate the intricacies of the human person—body and soul. This includes the masculinity and femininity of the body and soul. Masculinity doesn't just look like plain black suits and white shirts—it also looks like silk patterned button-downs, cable knit sweaters, peacoats, and yes, even pink suits.

In many Catholic circles, we encounter those who believe women should *only* wear dresses. Or that a woman is *more* feminine if she wears skirts, florals, pinks, etc. But we cannot buy into the belief that a garment can "make" someone feminine or masculine, or else we find ourselves in the same trap of the secular world which claims a man can wear women's clothing and "become" a woman in doing so. No garment can transform the essence of one's being. It can, however, highlight, complement, or emphasize the truth of one's being.

Part 3

PERSONAL STYLE AND YOU

THE DREADED MODESTY SECTION

*W*ell, if we are going to talk about the relationship between men and women, it was only a matter of time before we came to the topic of modesty. It seems like no female Catholic writer or speaker can escape without having to touch on modesty, let alone a Catholic fashion writer. I will admit that in the past, I have been frustrated with how this topic is handled in the Church. The significance of how a woman dresses is often solely focused on modesty, ignoring all of the wonderful opportunities we have to creatively share the uniqueness of the human person, made in the image of God.

But I will admit ... this topic is very important.

Modesty can be a topic people are either confused about, roll their eyes at, or are a little *too* enthusiastic about. I remember being told what not to wear as a kid—that definitely kick-started my rebellious teenage years. In fact, it landed me in a therapist's office for refusing to return a pair of especially tight jeans. Luckily for my mom, my obsession with weird fashion trends took the wheel and I was seen wearing plaid skirts *over* smells-like-teen-spirit-worthy jeans. I was, however, still on the receiving end of a few uncomfortable modesty "interventions."

When I was fifteen, I went to a parish dance where I was taken aside by a woman who said, "When you spin, your dress comes up above your knee." Me? The kid in a loose-fitting tube of fabric? In preparation for this dance, I had specifically chosen the unflattering tube dress *because* it was so painfully modest. The woman went on to tell me I should be "mindful that there were boys and priests in attendance" then gave me the option of changing or leaving, dropping a giant garbage bag full of prom dresses stolen from the set of *Napoleon Dynamite*. That was a hard thing for me to understand at fifteen, that a dress that was so clearly modest was being viewed as immodest, inappropriate, or tempting, as I didn't intend to be any of those things! I re-emerged (knees fully covered) in a different outfit, the equivalent of wearing the scarlet letter "A" at Catholic dances. There have been other instances when I was chastised and humiliated for wearing clothing that truly wasn't immodest or revealing in any way. And I say that honestly because I did intentionally cross the line at times, like dressing in a revealing Britney Spears costume for Halloween while my friends dressed like saints.

Thanks to years of studying the Theology of the Body, the truths revealed about the body have transformed how I dress from the inside out. Dressing "modestly" wasn't necessarily something I had to consciously remind myself of every day, but something that naturally happened because I had grown in understanding of my identity as someone made in God's image.

In years of observing how modesty is approached in Catholic circles, it is akin to slapping a Band-Aid on a giant gaping wound. "Follow these exact rules, and you will be modest," "Dress this way, and you will be a good girl." Somewhere along the way, we have lost the real message behind the significance of dressing with reverence toward the body, we've become obsessed with rules, and we've veered into scrupulosity. Modesty is a delicate topic that demands tact and a full understanding of the human person. But more times than not it's handled like a bull in a china shop, and it can have devastating effects on how real people regard their bodies and sexuality. Dressing modestly has turned into a warped hyper-modesty that can project personal struggles with scrupulosity, fear, impurity, and misunderstanding upon young women—harming them in the name of helping them. Oftentimes, these "interventions" leave young girls feeling confused, dirty, and, ironically, objectified.

As a result, many young girls have grown to view their very own bodies and sexuality in unhealthy ways. Think about it: if from a young age, girls are only counseled on whether they are clothed immodestly, we are inadvertently training them to look at ourselves from a third person perspective. In the worst cases, we are unknowingly teaching our little girls to look at themselves as an object, where their bodies are an enemy to themselves. I will never forget getting ready to go outside with my friends as little girls, and them anxiously fretting over whether their T-shirts showed too much of their collarbones. Or their aghast voices exclaiming, "*Lilly!*" while quickly pulling down my shirt that showed a sliver of my belly as we lounged alone in their bedrooms.

When not handled well, modesty can breed fear and hatred of one's own body. Girls and young women frantically wonder, "Am I being immodest?" "Will a man lust after me because of how I'm dressed?" "Am I leading men into sin?" "Do I look too sexy? Too showy? Do I look vain?" Constantly looking at themselves from the outside in, from a sexualized perspective. They are taught to anticipate and prevent the worst response from men and how they might see their bodies. This warps a girl's relationship with her body, which is already rocky to begin with. In extreme fear of sin, her body becomes an enemy to herself and her salvation, as well as the men who could be tempted by her. Talk about great responsibility at a young age.

In an attempt to be completely in the "safe" zone of modesty, many girls overcompensate by becoming obsessed with the rules of modesty and the exact inches of flesh our clothes must cover. Every day dressing becomes ruled by fear and doubt. "Am I being immodest? What's OK? What's not? Can I wear a skirt that goes above my knees? Shorts? Leggings?"

I've noticed that whenever I give talks or write about modesty, girls want exact measurements. They want to know exactly which garments are "allowed" and which aren't. One girl even asked me recently, "Can an outfit send me to hell?"

The problem with answering these girls is that there aren't clear-cut modesty guidelines. To make matters more confusing, different cultures, time periods, environments, and activities call for different levels of clothedness. What was considered immodest in the 1800s in Western countries is no longer seen as immodest now. Remember when showing an ankle was considered scandalous in the Victorian era? Context plays an important role as well. For example, wearing a bathing suit to the pool is appropriate, but wearing the same thing to the grocery store is inappropriate. Again, gymnasts and swimmers wear high-cut, skin-tight leotards that are necessary for their sport, but it doesn't make them scandalous.

Similarly, culture also determines what is "modest" or "immodest" for its people. Certain African countries don't bat an eye at exposed breasts, and the traditional Indian two-piece garment, Lehenga Choli, reveals a woman's midriff. Meanwhile, in Iran, women are obligated by law to veil themselves. What is modest relies heavily on external environmental factors and the specific culture in which one exists.

WHAT DOES THE CHURCH SAY ABOUT MODESTY?

It may come as a surprise that the Catholic Church does not have specific rules for the number of inches of fabric that must cover the body or where.

So what does the *Catechism of the Catholic Church* say? It addresses modesty in a way that doesn't command specific dressing rules but emphasizes the true purpose and significance of dressing to uphold the dignity of the human person:

- "There is a modesty of the feelings as well as of the body. It protests against the voyeuristic explorations of the human body in certain advertisements, or against the solicitations of certain media that go too far in the exhibition of intimate things. Modesty inspires a way of life which makes it possible to resist the allurements of fashion and the pressures of prevailing ideologies" (CCC 2522).

- "Modesty protects the intimate center of the person. It means refusing to unveil what should remain hidden ... It guides how one looks at others and behaves toward them in conformity with the dignity of persons and their solidarity" (CCC 2521).

- "Modesty exists as an intuition of the spiritual dignity proper to man. It is born with the awakening consciousness of being a subject. Teaching modesty to children and adolescents means awakening in them respect for the human person" (CCC 2525).

There are no official "modesty rules," which leaves it to the individual's discernment. So how come we have so many Catholic groups with strict modesty rules?

Some Catholic groups tend toward a more extreme understanding of modesty, getting their inspiration from the "Marylike Crusade," which was developed by Fr. Bernard Kunkel and later adopted by individuals in the Society of St. Pius X, as well as by groups not in communion with the pope, such as the Congregation of Mary Immaculate Queen.

These groups often use the following quotes from Pope Pius XI and Pope Pius XII to support their extreme approach to modesty:

- "Parents should also prevent their daughters from taking part in public drills and athletic contests. If the girls are obliged to take part in them, the parents must see to it that they wear a costume that is entirely modest, and must never permit them to appear in immodest dress."

- "They shall not admit to the schools or colleges girls who are given to immodest dress; and if any such have been admitted, they shall be dismissed unless they change their ways."

- "Nuns, in accordance with the Letter of 23 August 1928, of the Sacred Congregation of Religious, shall not admit to their colleges, schools, oratories, or amusement centers, nor allow to remain there any girls who do not observe Christian modesty in dress."

- "Girls and women who are immodestly dressed are to be refused Holy Communion and excluded from the office of sponsor in the sacraments of baptism and confirmation, and in proper cases are even to be excluded from the church."[64]

What is most concerning about these rules is the exclusion of girls and women from activities, organizations, and even the sacrament of Holy Communion who do not meet their standards of modesty. You might be wondering, "Well, what exactly *are* their standards of modesty?"

In his decree, Pope Pius XI states, "A dress cannot be called decent which is cut deeper than two fingers breadth under the pit of the throat; which does not cover the arms at least to the elbows; and scarcely reaches a bit beyond the knees."[65]

For some context, this decree was issued in 1928 as a reaction to the extreme change in women's dress due to the "flapper" movement of the 1920s.

MAKING SENSE OF MODESTY

So, can you wear something that will send you to hell? Well, what constitutes a mortal sin? For a sin to be mortal, it must meet three conditions (see CCC 1857):

• It must concern a gravely sinful action (i.e., "grave matter").

• It must be committed with the full knowledge that it is gravely sinful.

• It must be committed with deliberate consent (full consent of the will).

Can immodesty be a grave matter? Yes. But we must consider the extremity of the immodesty at hand. If a woman is walking around knowing that what she is wearing is an extreme violation of her own body's dignity and the dignity of others and has the specific *intention* of causing men to sin by lusting after her—that is serious. Mortal sins cannot be done accidentally. A person who commits a mortal sin is one who *knows* that their sin is grave but still deliberately commits the sin anyway. This means that mortal sins are premeditated by the sinner and thus are a conscious rejection of God's law and love. Usually, women who do wear immodest garments are not intentionally trying to diminish their dignity, or the dignity of those around them, and most of the time, have no clue what impact their clothes could have on others. Most church leaders would agree that wearing an outfit that exposes your arms and legs is *not* a grave matter.

The apparition of the Blessed Virgin at Fatima is also used to legitimize extreme rules of modesty. While there aren't any official sources that confirm this quote, Our Lady is attributed as saying to St. Jacinta: "Immodesty in dress can lead to the loss of immortal souls, and if gravely offensive, is a mortal sin for the wearer and occasion of sin for the beholder of immodest fashions. Sins caused by immodest fashions send to hell, or at least make worthy of hell's fire, the souls of many of those exposed to these fashions."

In response to this well-known quote, I agree that what we wear can have serious repercussions. And it's true, the fashion industry especially perpetuates a sexualized image of women for profit. There are many industries that solely exist off of the exploitation of women's bodies. This is a heinous violation against women that greatly impacts souls.

But again, we do not see a guideline on what exactly is modest. This quote does not offer a rule book on how many inches of fabric need to be covering our bodies. It does, however, allude to the fact that there are levels of severity when it comes to immodesty: "Immodesty in dress can lead to the loss of immortal souls, and if gravely offensive, is a mortal sin for the wearer and occasion of sin for the beholder of immodest fashions."

Some believe that because Our Lady was fully covered (ankle to wrist) during the apparition, that it's how all women are called to dress.

So, is the official rule of modesty to dress exactly like Mary did in Jerusalem or during her apparitions? Maybe we should first ask *why* Mary dressed the way she did during apparitions. At the end of her life, Our Lady was bodily assumed into heaven. I don't know about you, but it wouldn't make sense to me that any apparition of her would have her in modern clothing. It would similarly be strange if Jesus appeared in khakis and a button-down. Our Lady is Queen of Heaven, so of course she is going to be dressed in glorious regal garb. Also, the point of Our Lady's immaculate nature needs to be considered. Her body is *especially* holy, *especially* sacred. She was free from original sin, and she was the first Tabernacle of the Lord. Her body is not just any body.

Yes, our bodies are also sacred and temples of the Holy Spirit. We also have immense dignity to protect. To put it simply, Our Lady is different. Consider her Josephite marriage with her most chaste spouse, St. Joseph. We believe Our Lady is the perpetual, Immaculate Virgin, meaning her relationship with St. Joseph did not involve the conjugal act. Mary was free from original sin; her immaculate body was raised to an untouchable status of holiness. Her body was already given to God himself.

This does not, of course, mean that married couples are somehow unchaste because they engage in the conjugal act (on the contrary, actually); it just means that Our Lady and St. Joseph were raised to a higher status of holiness and unity that did not require sexual union. Just because Our Lady has appeared fully covered does not mean the female form is inherently lust-inducing. She is covered because she is raised to a particularly sacred status. Our Lady's covered body does not mean that *our* bodies are inherently lustful or bad.

I do want to repeat that, as women, we must be cautious as to how we dress. Lust and sexual sin *are* serious. Protecting ourselves from being occasions of sin *is* important. But this begs the question: What *is* an occasion of sin when it comes to how we dress? When considering guidelines that demand "eight inches past the knee" and "two finger widths from the throat," we must ask: are we sexualizing body parts that are not even sexual? It is understandable how exposed cleavage, tight leggings, short shorts, bikinis, tube tops, and the like, can cause the viewer to more vividly imagine or even see the outline of a woman's breasts and genitals. These parts of a woman are directly tied to her sexual organs and her intimate sexual nature, so it makes sense that clothing which reveals them can be problematic. It also makes sense that some garments which are so tight can lead the viewer to easily imagine what the wearer might look like naked. However, is this true of a knee? A shoulder? An upper arm? A calf? A cleavage-free chest?

What is the man's personal responsibility for guarding his own chastity? Women cannot be made to be responsible for protecting a man from lusting after a non-sexual body part. Many modesty arguments have been that no matter what, women need to be mindful helpers to their brothers in Christ. There are also some anti-modesty arguments that hold that men can find *anything* sexually arousing, even an ankle or a knee. At what point is it a "him" problem? What is the difference between "normal" temptation and perversion? Who is responsible for that, the viewer or the viewed? Or both?

The Sermon on the Mount is an important passage to remember when considering this question of responsibility. As Jesus tells the assembled crowd, "You have heard that it was said, 'You shall not commit adultery.' But I say to you that every one who looks at a woman lustfully has already committed adultery with her in his heart. If your right eye causes you to sin, pluck it out and throw it away; it is better that you lose one of your members than your whole body be thrown into hell" (Matthew 5:27-30).

Jesus appeals to men and how *they* look at women. He doesn't say, "If a woman's appearance causes you to lust, *she* has committed adultery in her heart and only *she* is going to hell."

In the Theology of the Body, St. John Paul II specifically dissects this passage to clarify two things:

- An individual is responsible for his own sin.

- No one is a victim of his bodily desires and passions. He is capable of purity when viewing the other because he has been made for union.

We are not irrational animals. We are not victims to the passions of the flesh. A man is not powerless against his sexual desire. He must learn to encounter a woman's body, her sexuality, her beauty, and not immediately be overcome by an animalistic desire to use her physically. The idea that it is the woman's responsibility to keep man from lusting after her is akin to the belief that the way a woman dresses is to blame for her sexual assault. The answer to man's lust cannot be a complete rejection of the female form, especially body parts that are not sexual.

Remember, a woman's body is beautiful and good, reflecting the good of its creation. We have to be mindful of approaching the female form in a manner of reverence, not in fear or shame.

Man can and must achieve a state of personal freedom to behold the goodness of woman's body, without letting himself become victim to his temptation. If we regard the female body as an occasion of sin to the point of concealing as much of it as possible, are we not feeding into a greater disconnect between man and woman?

IMMODESTY, A SYMPTOM OF A DEEPER PROBLEM

When reading documents or opinions on modesty which can be viewed as more extreme, the humanity of the "immodest" woman is often not addressed. Like I said earlier, the way in which modesty is handled can be likened to slapping a Band-Aid on a giant gaping wound.

We need to see actual immodesty, where a girl or woman is truly revealing too much, as a symptom. Immodesty is just an indicator of a greater issue—a manifestation of a fractured sense of self-worth. A woman who dresses in revealing clothing is seeking to heal a deeper wound in all the wrong ways. I know from personal experience that if I am in a place of brokenness—desiring to be wanted, known, seen, loved, and affirmed—then I am much more likely to seek that out through male affirmation. Sadly enough, the easiest way to immediately feel beautiful and wanted is to wear clothes that get cheap attention. It's like an addict who just needs a quick fix to feel better, even though they know it's not a real solution to their pain. The fact of the matter is we live in a broken world that not only teaches young girls that their value only comes from their sexuality, but women are also vulnerable to toxic familial or romantic relationships that breed trauma wounds. When the core of a woman is so badly damaged, the expectation of perfect modest dress is unfair. Excluding, rejecting, or having disdain for "immodest" women is the last thing that is going to help someone who is struggling to see themselves as valued, loved, and inherently wanted.

Almost all sin comes from a place of internal brokenness and a lack of knowledge of one's worth. Nobody desires sin for the sake of sinning. Anything bad that a person desires is a misguided expression of something *good* that a person was designed to desire. We don't just have an underlying evil nature that exists to drag us to hell. When we sin, it's because our *good* nature has been warped. When a woman dresses in a way that violates her own dignity, it's because she thinks she is going to receive love and affirmation. Often, she is not even aware of what she truly desires or how to get it, but she slips into dressing immodestly because she is so desperate to be fulfilled. She also is not aware of what she is sacrificing and how she's betraying herself through her actions. Unfortunately, many of us haven't had the formation to understand the fullness of our own identity.

A healthy application of modesty requires an understanding of the Theology of the Body. Before we intervene or reprimand someone for dressing a certain way, we need to remember that they are probably functioning from a broken space. I know that if someone expressed disgust or disdain for how I was dressing, it simply made me feel worse about myself. Even though someone might say, "I'm just criticizing how they're dressed, not them," consider the psychological relationship between one's physical identity and their clothing. It is an extension of themselves—even if it is a manifestation of their broken perspective of themselves. We must tread carefully.

THE FAMILIAR TRAP OF OBJECTIFICATION

St. John Paul II has been quoted as saying that the problem with pornography is not that it shows too much of the person but too little. Essentially, he means that this hyper-sexualized culture views a woman's body for her parts; she is nothing more than her body. When we solely focus on our own bodies or the bodies of others, we are not seeing ourselves or others for their whole personhood. We are only seeing them for their parts. This affront is most obvious when we consider things like prostitution, stripping, pornography, the Victoria's Secret fashion show. In these acts of degradation, a woman's body-soul unity is intimately attacked. It violates the sacredness of her identity, made in the image of God. The objectification of her body attempts to separate the very core of the woman's identity, making her personhood for "me," rather than a whole person who's called by God for eternity. In this act, she is an object for use, a body meant for consumption.

This is exactly what the extreme modesty crowd argues they are fighting against. But hyper-modesty can be viewed as the other side of this same coin of objectification.

With hyper-modesty, there is still an extreme focus on the body and a woman's sexuality. The argument of someone who subscribes to hyper-modesty might be that their goal *is* to truly emphasize the whole person, by not letting the body detract from the soul and by avoiding occasions of sin that the body might cause. But at its core is the implication that the body is bad and must be hidden.

You can equally objectify a woman's body through extreme modesty. When a woman is covering up every inch of her body to be modest, or someone is telling her to cover up every inch, it's feeding into the same message we are fighting against— namely, that a woman's body is made for consumption. It may sound crazy, but immodesty and hyper-modesty can be two sides of the same coin, extremes on opposite ends of one spectrum.

When we become obsessed with modesty, we are treating the female body as something that *is* meant to be lusted after. Let's break this down in plain terms:

Immodesty: A woman's body is made for use, so use it.

Hyper-modesty: A woman's body is made for use, so hide it.

When a woman is told to hide every curve, cover every inch, and disguise her body to avoid men lusting after her, we are unwittingly believing the same idea that *Playboy, Cosmopolitan,* and the *Sports Illustrated* Swimsuit Edition promote—a woman's body is an object inherently made for consumption. Without a doubt, our culture is extremely sexualized. The Devil attacks what is most important in society—human life, family, gender, and in particular, the woman. The exploitation of female sexuality has led the way for the crumbling of society. Because of this constant visual reminder of the objectification and perversion of sex in our media, many of us have fallen into the subconscious belief that sex is perverted and the body is bad, that the body and sex are an enemy to us and our salvation. I have heard many married women share how hard it was for them to rewire their brains beginning on their wedding night after years of viewing sex as bad and dirty and their bodies as occasions of sin. This is a falsehood that many Catholics are psychologically dealing with.

In our Catholic culture, a common response to the problem is to just avoid the topic of sex entirely, partially because secular culture abuses it so much. Parents see pornography-drenched media and their response is to pretend it's not there because they're afraid and embarrassed to talk about sex. Sex has become associated with dirtiness, use, and objectification, rather than a culture of life, goodness, love, and unity. The avoidant approach to sex just feeds into the subconscious belief that sex=bad and body=bad.

There are some Catholic communities where the women, afraid of being immodest, intentionally dress in clothing that deemphasizes the female form. But see, they are onto something. There is an underlying acknowledgement that a woman's beauty *is* tied to her sexuality. For them, to avoid sexual attention means also hiding one's beauty as well. But a woman's beauty is tied to her sexuality because that is exactly how God made her. A woman's beauty is a sign of her physically creative nature, her ability to bear life within her. As we have seen earlier, feminine beauty has an evangelizing power, drawing mankind to contemplate the divine.

Because feminine beauty and sexuality are so intimately connected to new life, the Devil has attacked it viciously in our culture. Unfortunately, in an effort to protect ourselves from objectification, many of us have simply thrown out the baby with the bathwater. The answer isn't to ignore, hide, or throw away feminine sexuality. We should not discard this God-given gift of beauty out of fear.

REVERENCE > MODESTY

The word "modesty" has a lot of baggage attached to it. We have the history of the Marylike Crusade and negative personal experiences of "interventions." But maybe modesty isn't the right word for describing this internal transformation we're trying to promote?

So let's break down what the word modesty actually means.

The first definition: "The quality or state of being unassuming or moderate in the estimation of one's abilities."

The second definition: "Behavior, manner, or appearance intended to avoid impropriety or indecency."

The second definition of modesty, which is the one we associate the most with the term, is to avoid indecency and scandal. When using this definition of modesty as a blanket term for women's dress, it implies a woman's body as something negative because it needs to be kept in check or else it will lead to impropriety or sin. Overall, this definition of modesty is meant to be a reminder of the potential negative outcome of dressing a certain way. It's a reminder of how *not* to dress. Maybe this is another reason why the "modesty movement" often elicits eyerolls and exasperated sighs. I think most Catholics and Christians can agree that the mission to dress with dignity is important, but the packaging has become weighed down with negativity.

This is why I choose to use the word "reverence" over "modesty." This word implies a positive truth about the female body, rather than negativity. Reverence reminds us of the highly esteemed status of our feminine bodies, the evangelizing beauty we carry within us, the privilege of being co-creators with God, and the dignity that is due to us specifically as women. I am much more excited and motivated to take care of this gift of being a woman when I am called to have reverence for my body. At the center of all of this is the need to reclaim reverence for sex in general, which will lead to the respect for feminine and masculine sexuality, rather than exploitation or fear.

A friend once wisely said, "If you don't understand sex, you don't understand anything." He was right. If we do not understand the deeply unitive, sacred meaning of sex, we don't understand the human person. Period. If we don't understand the spousal union as an image of the divine communion of persons in the Trinity, we don't understand our own anthropology or our purpose as individuals made for eternity. We are made to give the gift of self. In the spousal union, our bodies make gift manifest. At the core of our identity, we were made body and soul, in God's image. Not understanding how we were made and what we were made for is not understanding who *we* are or who God is. This is why objectification is such a crime against our humanity; as the antithesis of gift, it attempts to destroy and obscure our very identity and God's image within all of us.

To heal the wounds of objectification, we must reconstruct or restore any deeply rooted misunderstandings of the human body and sex. For every negative encounter of something sexually perverse, there needs to be a multitude of conversations with people on the beauty and significance of this essential God-given gift of sex. We need to do this so Catholic men and women don't grow up with a subconscious inclination to view sex and the human body as something that's perverse or dirty, leading to a complete misunderstanding of the human person overall. This requires parents, couples, and single young men and women to really dive into the teachings of the Theology of the Body, so they may first educate themselves and eradicate any false beliefs of the body. Once we have a truly Catholic understanding of our own anthropology, we are much more equipped to teach others and have healthy conversations regarding modesty.

The Theology of the Body is so incredibly crucial because at its core it's an explanation of the worth of each individual human person. And that is exactly why it's the answer to so many wounds in our culture. For a woman to dress modestly out of a place of true personal freedom, she must have a clear understanding of her worth. When we think of the pains of low self-esteem, sexual exploitation, abuse, toxic relationships, and even things like violence, the source of it is a lack of understanding of the worth of the human person—whether it be yourself or someone else. These symptoms all begin with the core wound of not knowing one's worth.

In St. John Paul II's work, we see how Jesus tells us our worth. None of us was created by accident but *intentionally*. The Creator of the universe specifically thought of you, everything that you are, in all of your uniqueness and unrepeatability, and wanted you to exist forever. We were made for unity with each other because we were first made for unity with God.

Whenever I address young women, I try to express the magnitude of what their existence means. That the Creator of life itself—the same God who made the stars and galaxies, the seas and oceans teeming with life, the mountains that pierce the clouds, watercolor sunsets, unrepeatable snowflakes, fiery landscapes of foliage in autumn, the God who breathes life into every living thing—wants *you* to exist. In all of the endlessly beautiful creations the eye can behold, you are far more beautiful and important in his eyes. So important that Jesus Christ literally died for *you*. He thought of you from the beginning, thought of you as he died on the cross, and thinks of you at every moment. When he created humanity, this act was not just some mass production of human life but he willed *you* to exist. When Jesus died on the cross, you weren't just an unknown face amid billions; he thought of *you* as he died on the cross. He aches for *you* to join him for all eternity. Jesus' love for you is personal.

When we know who we are in relation to the Creator, our entire life changes. We do not embark on this journey of learning our worth so we may meet arbitrary modesty rules but so that our entire lives may be transformed. The goal is this knowledge of one's true identity, not dressing a certain way.

This is what I mean by addressing the core wound, not the symptom. Immodesty is a symptom of a broken sense of worth. We need to begin by educating women on this truth of their identity. When you have a strong understanding of being made in the image of God, it pours out of you in every way. You finally see yourself through a true lens, not one obscured by shallow industries, pop culture, media, trends, or earthly successes. The more you see yourself through God's eyes, the more you view yourself with love, reverence, charity, and honesty. Naturally, this impacts how you move through life—loving those around you, finding yourself in the gift of self. When you know that you were made in his likeness, your entire life shifts. The way you express yourself is transformed, including how you dress. Dressing with reverence is something you eventually don't even think about, but subconsciously do. It is simply a part of the package.

Of course, discovering your worth is not a one-stop destination you stay at permanently. It is something we are constantly having to re-learn, reaffirm, and re-discover. I can't tell you how many times in my life I have felt so assured in my true identity and let it transform how I expressed myself, only to hit a road bump caused by previous trauma, forgetfulness, cultural influence, and found myself insecure and dressing immodestly for affirmation. Discovering our infinite value is a lifelong journey which the Devil is always trying to sabotage. The point is that we keep fighting, we keep getting back up again, we keep striving to repair our skewed vision of self so we may live more fully.

SO WHAT IS MODEST DRESS, THEN?

You might be thinking, "OK, well that is all well and good on a philosophical level, but what does modest dress actually look like?" At the end of the day, we need concrete tips, examples, and explanations. We know that modest dress begins within, but we can also reaffirm to ourselves our worth by wearing things that reinforce that truth.

I am not here to lay down rules, give measurements, or condemn specific garments. Much of modesty has to do with balance and the overall picture which is being communicated. For example, I was not allowed to wear spaghetti straps growing up. They were the forbidden fruit of my youth. As an adult, do I think spaghetti straps are immodest or too revealing? No. That said, I wouldn't wear a skintight spaghetti strap top with tight pants or short shorts, but I would wear spaghetti straps in the form of a long, billowing dress, loose tank, or paired with looser pants. Context also plays an important role. I would not wear spaghetti straps to church (though I made this uncomfortable mistake once at an ordination Mass!). Similarly, do I think crop tops are inherently lust-inducing? No. But would I wear a crop top with low-rise jeans? No, but I would wear a tasteful crop top paired with a high-waisted skirt or pants. It is all about balance.

Still, I appeal to the interior of the woman by challenging her to ask, "Why am I wearing this?" Intention plays a major role in modesty. Whether we realize it or not, when we put on an outfit, we are hoping to elicit a response or to be noticed by those around us. The body is not inherently bad or lustful, but we can have intentions that use our bodies in ways that betray its dignity. The way we physically express ourselves is a manifestation of how we see ourselves and how we want others to see us. Even as an adult, I still find myself wearing things with the wrong intentions.

Sure, we can delude ourselves and make excuses for dressing a certain way, but I think we all know when we are wearing something to get male attention or affirmation. If you stopped me in the mall whilst I was wearing booty shorts and a crop top and asked, "What are you getting out of wearing this?" in answering honestly, I would admit that I was getting a boost of confidence from men looking at me. And look, we all fall into this trap. It feels good to be seen as attractive. But if we were to dig deeper into that attention and ask, "Does it feel good to be seen *only* for your body? Does anyone have a right to use you in their minds? Does this shallow physical affirmation solve your subconscious belief that you are not enough? How long does it take for that confidence buzz to wear off before you need another hit?" We should always ask ourselves, "What void is this attention filling? What do I really want?"

We can trick ourselves into thinking that we are OK with being used (either physically or mentally) if we are getting that shallow confidence boost in return. But is any confidence real if it solely depends on other people? Wouldn't true confidence be unmovable, independent of others, regardless of whether you were getting affirmation? Confidence is not derived from people who do not know or care about you or are simply using you for their own pleasure. We derive confidence from the fact that we are loved by the people who see us as whole beings, flaws included. This love is an extension of God, who loves us unconditionally.

In her song "Young and Beautiful," Lana Del Rey ponders unconditional love. She speaks to the deep yearning present in every single woman's heart—to be loved, to be enough, no matter what she looks like. A woman wants to know that her value isn't in her body, but who she is as a person. We all ache for this knowledge of our identity. But when we lack confidence, we often turn to this need to look sexually appealing to affirm to ourselves, "Well, I must have worth if I am desired." This is why I challenge women to honestly ask themselves, "Why am I wearing this? What am I trying to prove and to whom? What am I hoping to get out of wearing this? Am I just seeking attention? Will this truly satisfy or add to the ache in my heart?" We then need to move forward by asking ourselves what we actually want to communicate about our identity—and this is where personal style comes in.

WHAT PERSONAL STYLE IS *NOT*

You may have already gathered this, but personal style is not about clothing. It is about understanding your identity as someone made in the image and likeness of God. I wouldn't want anyone's final takeaway after reading this book to be: "I need to buy a bunch of new things or look a certain way." So, let's just start this chapter with what personal style is *not* about.

So many style books revolve around formulas of "what colors flatter you the most; what body type are you?" Tests for figuring out whether you are a "cool spring," "warm summer," or if your body is shaped like an hourglass, pear, heart, etc. They tell you to "wear this, not that," or narrow down your personal style to "types"—romantic, classic, relaxed, sporty. Sure, these things might be helpful to some, but oftentimes it makes personal style feel rule bound. It isn't. Sometimes in the pursuit of finding our style, we become slaves to being "flattered." We end up feeling like there are certain colors, silhouettes, and garments that we absolutely cannot wear because it is for a different body type or skin tone. We wonder if the things we love or feel drawn to are not for us.

One time I wore hot pink eyeshadow for a photo shoot. At the end of the day, I met a woman who said, "I don't think that's very flattering." She did not say this in a hostile tone but in an almost confessional one, as if she felt a duty to tell me. I replied matter-of-factly, "I don't care." She was surprised at my response, thinking I was offended and defensive but really, I just wanted to share that I truly didn't care if it wasn't flattering. Yes, a different eyeshadow would have brought out my eyes better, but I didn't want to wear it. I wanted to wear pink eyeshadow.

Like other women who grew up in the 1990s and 2000s, I was inundated with magazines, articles, and books on how to dress to flatter myself. The sole purpose of dressing was to look as physically good as possible—to reach our greatest physical potential by looking our absolute best all the time. The goal was to have a wardrobe of flattering hues, with clothes that perfectly emphasized our socially acceptable body parts and de-emphasized the unacceptable ones, to have haircuts that accentuate our bone structure, and highlights that didn't wash us out. I even wrote articles about these very things as a magazine editor. But I got to a point where I didn't want to keep telling women that their bodies needed to be more "flattered," that their body shape, weight, and proportions were unattractive and needed to be "balanced" out, aka detracted from. I couldn't in good conscience tell women that something was wrong with their God-given bodies.

People will argue, "OK, but there's truth to the fact that equal proportions are beautiful. The golden ratio! Beauty is not subjective! There are actual measurements that point toward beauty!" My question is this: At what cost are we willing to hold actual people—real human beings—to this rigid standard? At what point do we realize we're treating multi-faceted individuals as objects, like malleable mounds of clay that need to be molded into perfect proportions to have value? These "body type" articles or books shroud themselves in a righteous mission of helping women to feel more confident in their own skin, but often perpetuate the belief that we are only as good as when we look "our best" or as close to physically perfect as possible. Ironically, this just exacerbates the issue of women seeing themselves as just bodies, not whole beings. The purpose of a woman's physical appearance isn't looking "perfect." We do not exist to be the best physical versions of ourselves every day. We do not exist to attain the "golden ratio" or specific standard of beauty. We exist to be who God made us to be as unrepeatable beings. And this is exactly why I believe authentic personal style is important. Personal style is not about fashion, physical perfection, having the right clothes, always making the "right" impression, following trends, or looking a certain way. Personal style is about growing in understanding of your identity, plain and simple.

Personal style actually requires a healthy detachment from placing too much focus on and value in one's appearance. True freedom within personal style means joyfully expressing the beauty of your body–soul unity, separate from the influence and pressure of others' opinions and judgment. Some of the most inspiring examples of personal style are the outfits that come from a place of pure creativity and carefree self-expression. Yes, that means throwing on the kooky Hawaiian shirt with the polka dot skirt, experimenting with bright colors and prints, wearing those bizarro 1980s embroidered pants, and having fun with this expression of self because you know your worth comes from God, not the superficial opinions or standards of the world.

This might sound contrary to what we have been conditioned to think style means, but there needs to be an element of apathy when it comes to getting dressed. Let's reflect on Matthew 6:25–34 to shed some light:

> "Therefore I tell you, do not be anxious about your life, what you shall eat or what you shall drink, nor about your body, what you shall put on. Is not life more than food, and the body more than clothing? Look at the birds of the air: they neither sow nor

reap nor gather into barns, and yet your heavenly Father feeds them. Are you not of more value than they? And which of you by being anxious can add one cubit to his span of life? And why are you anxious about clothing? Consider the lilies of the field, how they grow; they neither toil nor spin; yet I tell you, even Solomon in all his glory was not arrayed like one of these. But if God so clothes the grass of the field, which today is alive and tomorrow is thrown into the oven, will he not much more clothe you, O men of little faith? Therefore do not be anxious, saying, 'What shall we eat?' or 'What shall we drink?' or 'What shall we wear?' For the Gentiles seek all these things; and your heavenly Father knows that you need them all. But seek first his kingdom and his righteousness, and all these things shall be yours as well. Therefore do not be anxious about tomorrow, for tomorrow will be anxious for itself. Let the day's own trouble be sufficient for the day."

Is this not the most comforting Bible passage ever? This passage is about perspective and priorities. The things we concern ourselves with and worry over are often things in which we place an undue amount of worth. Our Lord in the Gospel of Matthew reminds us that our worth comes from God, not in the worldly things we think we need or what we think defines us. He clarifies, "All these things the pagans seek." Trust me, I have been there. Those of us who do not have our identity solidified in God seek things of the world for fulfillment. We seek to be made in the image of the world, rather than in God's. We mistakenly believe the perfect body and the right clothes will bring us an understanding of our ultimate purpose. Of course, these things never do. When we chase them, we feel empty. Or worse, we are simply too distracted to let ourselves even feel the pain of our emptiness. In the above passage from Matthew, Jesus assures us that the Father knows we need food, clothing, and healthy bodies to live, but that we will never find him in the pursuit of those things alone. We have to place these things in a value hierarchy to inform how we should pursue these things. We must first seek the kingdom of heaven before all things. Basically, we need to sort out our priorities.

FEMININITY DOESN'T EQUAL PHYSICAL PERFECTION

In some Christian fashion circles, women encourage each other to get dressed up every day, to put on makeup, to put in that effort even when you do not feel like it because "you deserve it." This is a nice sentiment, and I am sure that it has helped many women. However, the problem with this message is that we lose that human element of imperfection, to say nothing of the recognition of one's worth without clothing and makeup. You don't need clothing or makeup to prove your worth to yourself, or anyone else. The picture that's painted on these Instagram grids and stories are of seemingly perfect women, who just "have it together." We rarely see filter-less photos of blemishes, messy hair, lived-in ensembles, or relatable captions. Instead, the images are almost solely aspirational; women floating around in dresses, soft pink light filtering through the lens, flowers in hand, perfectly done makeup, and captions with tidy quotes on femininity. And when someone gains enough attention or followers for the image they're creating and attaching to a message on how women "should" look or behave, it can perpetuate the same pop-culture problem that insists a woman's appearance must be a certain way; in other words, that women must "look perfect." Again, we can face that familiar trap of self-objectification when we focus so much on our appearance.

Being a woman should not be tied to a narrow concept of what is visually "perfect." Femininity is not a kitsch version of what is beautiful. It is not sickeningly sweet or saccharine. It is Caravaggio; it is real, human. My childhood friend, Veronica, said to me, "The ultimate image of femininity is Our Lady, who, at the foot of the cross, beheld her son. A sword pierced her heart. She bore immense suffering. She must have been covered in dirt, sweat, blood, and tears." What happened to this deeply human element of the beauty of femininity? The beauty of bearing great suffering? Are we not at peak femininity when we unite our suffering with God? Are we not most feminine when we push our babies into the world, sweating, screaming, crying? Are we not most feminine when we are running around after our children all day, exhausted, unshowered, covered in their mess? Are we not most feminine when we bear pain, offering our heartache to Christ? Are we not most feminine when we are simply … women?

For years I believed this lie that to be feminine I needed to "look" perfect, until I realized it did not actually help me understand my inherent value. I also realized that perpetuating this image does not help other women either. This became crystal clear to me when I lost my job at the magazine, moved back home from my super cool Manhattan life, and was flat broke. Instead of wearing carefully curated outfits and a face full of makeup, I was existing in dilapidated sweats and messy buns. My flaws were on full display. I had lost all of the physical things that were bolstering my confidence. For the first time in a long time, I stood before God in my most raw form. I wasn't "NYC Lilly," "Fashion

Lilly," "Cool outfit Lilly," or "Pretty Lilly." I was just Lilly. So there I was, feeling worthless because I didn't "look" perfect anymore.

But the answer to discovering your worth is not found by putting on makeup or a stylish outfit. That's a Band-Aid. What's required is digging deeper into that ugly place you so desperately fear within yourself, your most flawed self, and realizing you have worth regardless. That you are loved, no matter how imperfect you are. Going out in my sweats, with pimples exposed, and four-day hair challenged me to discover that my worth was in God, not my appearance. I allowed myself to be seen on social media looking greasy, tired, my mouthguard in, wearing old T-shirts. Let me tell you, I grew in confidence as "raw" Lilly because I decided to commit to the truth that I had worth no matter how I looked. That I am enough as an imperfect woman. Some women condemn being seen in sweatpants and without makeup, claiming it's a part of the culture's disintegration into "sloppiness." But being a human is not perfect. Sometimes it's sloppy and messy. But we, and others, deserve love and respect regardless. We have worth and dignity, no matter how we look.

For me, allowing myself to be "raw" and imperfect grounds my identity in God, and similarly, so do my more creative outfits. When you are wearing something that is a bit "out there," there is that crucial element of not caring about the perception of the world. I have learned to not care about the sideways glances, the frowns, the questioning faces, or laughs. This prepares me for other ways I might not be accepted and to learn to be OK with that. As Catholics, we are not trying to fit in with the world where it is trendy to wear certain things or trendy to believe certain things. We are called to be countercultural and to be affirmed in the beatitudes. Ironically enough, my out-of-this-world outfits remind me that I am not made for this world, and

I don't need to fit in. Ironically enough, the key to tapping into your personal style and the knowledge of your worth means caring less about how you look. I mean, don't we feel farther from God when we obsess over our appearance? Isn't that what that passage in the Gospel of Matthew was trying to get at? And before anyone jumps down my throat, I don't mean being careless. I mean "care less," not careless. I don't mean personal neglect or complete disrespect for the beautiful way God made us. I mean being healthily detached from the toxic belief that our worth comes from how we look and actively keeping ourselves grounded in this truth. When we are less obsessed about our appearance, we are able to focus on those around us. We are able to focus less on ourselves and be present to the people God has placed in our lives. We are able to give ourselves. The hierarchy of values is the ability to order our priorities correctly.

HOW TO DEVELOP YOUR PERSONAL STYLE

After all of this you might be wondering, "OK, so where do I even begin with developing my personal style?" Like, "Hello? Tangible tips, please!" The goal of this book is to explain the theory behind why style is important, to validate it as an expression of self and the theological implications of that. To give truly helpful advice for developing your personal style, it would require photos and videos (shameless plug to follow me on social media to get that kind of help). But I am going to do my best to give you the basics!

We have been raised to believe that all we need is a movie-worthy makeover scene and voila, new identity unlocked! But really, it is a stripping back, not an adding on, process. Let's begin by saying that personal style is exactly that, a process. It is not an end goal you "achieve" and simply wake up one day perfectly expressing yourself through your clothes. Remember when all it took for Andy Sachs (in *The Devil Wears Prada*) was access to the *Vogue* closet and style advice from Stanley Tucci? Unfortunately, it is not as simple or affordable as free designer clothes. At thirty, I am still developing my style. I remember being fifteen and thinking that all I needed was a hundred dollars and a trip to the mall for an entirely new wardrobe. One visit to Hollister for a pair of bedazzled jeans proved that belief to be very wrong. In the world of fast fashion, it sort of feels like it should be as easy as that. But really, the process is a lot more fun, experimental, affordable, and personal. Hey, would you look at that! Personal style is personal!

Here are five pillars for developing your personal style. This is the beginning of the process, to prepare yourself for further growth as you learn what best expresses your identity.

1. Detox fast fashion

Quitting fast fashion is a lot like quitting sugar. At first it hurts, you crave it like crazy, and then after a while you aren't even attracted to it anymore. Three months into my decision to quit fast fashion, a friend asked me if I would stop in Zara with her. I was nervous entering the store. Would I feel the "I gotta have it!" compulsion? Weirdly enough, I felt nothing. It was as if a veil had been lifted and I was finally seeing the clothes for what they were: clothing that didn't reflect who I really am. I didn't even like them anymore.

When we solely shop fast fashion, we don't allow ourselves to develop taste. We suppress the thing inside of us that appreciates art and beauty, because we are letting an industry tell us what's "cool" or "relevant." Taking yourself off the fast fashion diet gives your brain a second to think for itself. I personally felt like I was finally discovering what I actually liked. So do yourself a favor and stop shopping trends. Let your brain do a reset so you can get back in touch with what you are actually drawn to. Similarly, unfollow trendy fashion influencers who all look the same and keep shoving products in your face. Give your palate a break so your taste can emerge!

2. Build your wardrobe foundation

My closet used to be jam-packed with super bold, kooky, vibrant garments. They were all "statement" pieces. I regularly found myself staring into my multicolored, multi-textured closet and panicking about having nothing to wear. Here's the thing: I had nothing to wear because I didn't have any basic items to wear *with* my statement items.

To develop your personal style, your wardrobe needs a strong foundation of basic, classic items. Garments that are neutral, versatile, and easy to build upon. Think of these items like a canvas and your personal style as the painting. For example, plain vintage jeans, black pants, bias cut skirts, midi skirts, blazers, trench coats, relaxed button downs, denim jackets, plain tees, turtleneck sweaters, black boots, ballet flats, oxfords, or any items within this realm of versatility. Also, look for styles in these garments that are classic—that is, the overall look hasn't changed a ton since its invention. For example, a classic trench coat in 2023 looks the same as it did in 1940. Similarly, a pair of straight-leg, midrise, bootcut Levi's also bear their trademark look as when they were originally created. Choose foundational items that stand the test of time! That way, you will keep them forever. For shopping, I recommend going to the thrift store before hitting the shops. Since these items are more classic and have been made and remade for the past few decades, you'll be able to find tons of secondhand, high-quality garments in great condition.

While they might not be as exciting as bright colors and patterns, choose these foundational items in neutral tones of black, white, cream, navy, and gray. Don't worry, they will end up emphasizing your expressive items!

3. Create an inspiration board

This is the oldest tip in the book. But come on, you already know you have a Pinterest account. Start doing some image research on style icons from the past and today. Type in terms like, "Classic style icon" and see what comes up. Do you find yourself drawn to anyone in particular? What about their outfits do you like? Or perhaps dislike? Look at the styles of Audrey Hepburn, Jane Birkin, Francois Hardy, and Jackie O, but also reference modern style icons like Zoe Kravitz, Iris Apfel, Olivia Palermo, Zendaya, Alexa Chung, or Jenny Walton. I also search "street style photography" on Pinterest; this will bring up authentic outfits, put together by very cool, everyday women.

Start pinning away and once you have a bunch on your board, put on your Sherlock Holmes hat and make connections between the looks. Is there a certain type of item you keep pinning? What descriptive terms come to your mind when considering all these photos together? Is there a color scheme that's emerging? Or a certain decade these looks are inspired by? Does the identity of any of the women you are inspired by resonate with you? Why might that be? Which garments would also reflect your unique identity? How could you put your own spin on it? Now, how would you incorporate those items (or items like them) into your lifestyle? Imagine yourself wearing them. Would you feel comfortable and like yourself?

4. Experiment

When developing your personal style, give yourself the freedom to experiment. Don't take the process too seriously. This should be *fun*. Stop telling yourself, "I could never pull that off." You are searching for items that express the beauty of *your* soul; who cares what other people think? Allow items to jump out at you—no matter how un-trendy or weird they may seem. Allow yourself to be drawn to unique fabrics, cuts, and designs. Imagine how you might mix and match those items with what you already own or your basic items. Again, I recommend shopping at the thrift store when you are experimenting. You will find one-of-a-kind garments, but they will not be a significant investment. You can also experiment by trading items with friends and sisters! Put your own interpretation on their clothes and give them a spin for a week to see if you feel comfortable in them. Reflect on how this test run of outfits impacted you every day. Check in with yourself to see if you are feeling more confident and self-assured. Note whether you feel relaxed in your outfit or fussy over details. Were you excited to get dressed every day?

When you are embarking on the process of developing your style, enter the thrift store, vintage shop, or any store with low expectations and with an open mind. Oftentimes, when you go in with a rigid idea of what you want, you can become defeated and give up on finding it. Don't close yourself off to things that you might not realize you love just yet! As silly as it sounds, let the clothes speak to you. Don't first think, "Is this practical?" Experimenting is all about tapping into your basic "I like it" or "I don't like it" reaction to certain styles of items.

5. Forgive yourself

I have put together a lot of funny looking outfits over the years. One time, I accidentally dressed like Peter Pan for a whole day in college. I didn't realize it until I took a second look at the green-on-green ensemble with cloth booties after classes. Did I feel embarrassed? Nah. Having fun with your style and trying different looks is all a part of the process! Also, it helps to be detached from the good ol' ego—it allows you to be more forgiving of yourself, to laugh at your mess ups, and move forward without letting it define you. Remember, your clothing can help express your identity—but *you* are not your clothes.

Do not judge yourself too harshly for a genuine effort to express beauty and creativity. Hopefully, this less critical approach to dressing will impact other areas of your life, helping you to be more charitable, understanding, and forgiving in other ways you are pursuing personal growth. Remember, your style is a reflection of your interior self—it grows *with* you. Be kind to yourself as you work on becoming who God has called you to be. And that is the point really, continuing to work on living out and expressing who you were made to be.

In conclusion, developing your personal style isn't an immediate makeover, but neither is your internal development. So be patient. Let it grow naturally and authentically. As cheesy as it sounds, personal style is not a destination, but a journey. Your style will evolve with you as you grow because the things you wear will reflect who you are as an ever-changing, evolving person.

Conclusion

THE REAL PURPOSE OF PERSONAL STYLE

Personal style is meant to aid the big picture—your journey toward Jesus Christ. The way you dress does not and cannot define your worth, but the way you dress can help you understand your worth. Sounds kind of confusing? Think of it like this: personal style is a tool for growing in understanding of your identity. It doesn't define who you are. You come first; clothes come later. You inform the outfit with your identity; the outfit does not inform your identity. Our identity comes from God, always. How you choose to express that is an opportunity to see yourself as God sees you, to know yourself as he *knows* you. The goal is to recognize how he has imbued your being with an infinite worth, guiding you to seek out the source of that love. As humans on this finite earth, we can only grasp at how we are made in his image. In our everyday lives, we are constantly seeking the origin of our being. We see this in our desire for union, our need for connection, and our attraction to beauty. How we physically express ourselves can serve as an aid in this lifelong pursuit of Christ, but we will only truly understand who we are as his beloved once we are with him for all eternity— partaking in the beatific vision for which we were made.

Forget about the "cool" "fancy" or "stylish" wardrobe. Forget about becoming a "new" version of yourself. Just focus on how you can grow in the understanding of how you were made.

Focus on becoming who you have always been called to be—yourself. Express the beauty of your soul through your style and dignify your body through your clothing. Treat your time developing your style like an unveiling process, discovering how God sees you through every garment you choose. Imagine how he formed you, the traits he delights in, how he smiles when he sees you rejoicing in how he made you.

Notes

1. John Paul II, "The Meaning of Original Solitude" in *Man and Woman He Created Them: A Theology of the Body* (Boston: Pauline, 2006), 7:2. Henceforth listed as TOB.

2. John Paul II, "Man in the Dimension of Gift," in TOB 14:4.

3. TOB 19:4.

4. John Paul II, *Urbi et Orbi* message, December 25, 1978, 1, vatican.va.

5. John Paul II, *Letter to Artists*, December 25, 1999, 1, vatican.va.

6. *Letter to Artists*, 1.

7. *Letter to Artists*, 12.

8. *Letter to Artists*, 6.

9. *Letter to Artists*, 2.

10. *Letter to Artists*, 12.

11. *Letter to Artists*, 14.

12. *Letter to Artists*, 12.

13. *Letter to Artists*, 10.

14. *Letter to Artists*, 2.

15. Thomas Carlyle, *Sartor Resartus* (1896), 28.

16. TOB 14:4.

17. https://www.eonline.com/news/1315892/rachel-zoe-shares-the-trends-set-to-take-over-in-2022

18. Hermann Lotze, *Microcosmus* (1885), 592.

19. *Microcosmus*, 93.

20. *Microcosmus*, 595.

21. *Microcosmus*, 595.

22. William James, *The Principles of Psychology* (1890), Vol. 1, 193.

23. Henry James, *The Portrait of a Lady* (1882), 205.

24. *Microcosmus*, 590.

25. *Letter to Artists*, 13.

26. *Urbi et Orbi*, 1.

27. *Letter to Artists*, 12.

28. TOB 19:4.

29. *Letter to Artists*, 5.

30. TOB 7:2.

31. TOB 6:3.

32. TOB 6:3.

33. TOB 7:1.

34. TOB 9:4.

35. TOB 5:5.

36. TOB 9:4.

37. TOB 19:5.

38. TOB 5:2.

39. TOB 10:1.

40. TOB 9:3.

41. TOB 9:3.

42. Second Vatican Council, *Gaudium et Spes* (1965), 2, vatican.va.

43. TOB 11:1.

44. *Letter to Artists*, 2.

45. *Letter to Artists*, 1.

46. *Letter to Artists*, 2.

47. Alice von Hildebrand, *The Privilege of Being a Woman* (San Francisco: Ignatius, 2005), 50.

48. Hildebrand, 59.

49. Hildebrand, 49.

50. Hildebrand, 41.

51. Hildebrand, 61.

52. TOB 21:5.

53. Hildebrand, 39.

54. Hildebrand, 51.

55. Hildebrand, x.

56. TOB 26:4.

57. TOB 26:8.

58. TOB 29:2.

59. TOB 29:2.

60. TOB 32:6.

61. TOB 32:6.

62. Second Vatican Council, *Gaudium et Spes* (1965), 2.

63. TOB 22:4.

64. Excerpts from the Letter of the Sacred Congregation of the Council (now the Sacred Congregation for the Clergy) to the world (Rome: *Acta Apostolicae Sedis*, 1930), 22.

65. Issued by the cardinal vicar of Rome (Basilio Pompili) for Pope Pius XI, September 24, 1928.